BUILDING SYSTEMS DESIGN SERIES

Volume III: Domestic Plumbing Design

BUILDING SYSTEMS DESIGN SERIES

Volume III: Domestic Plumbing Design

Jack L. Burton

Prentice Hall

Upper Saddle River, New Jersey   *Columbus, Ohio*

Library of Congress Cataloging-in-Publication Data

Burton, Jack L.
    Domestic plumbing design / Jack L. Burton.
        p.   cm. — (Building systems design series ; v. 3)
    Includes bibliographical references and index.
    ISBN 0-13-914029-8
    1. Plumbing. I. Title. II. Series.
  TH6123.B87   2000
  696′.1—dc21   99-29976
                                                        CIP

Editor: Ed Francis
Production Editor: Christine M. Buckendahl
Production Coordinator: Karen Fortgang, *bookworks*
Design Coordinator: Karrie Converse-Jones
Text Designer: STELLARViSIONs
Cover Designer: Jeff Vanik
Production Manager: Patricia A. Tonneman
Marketing Manager: Chris Bracken

This book was set in New Century Schoolbook by STELLARViSIONs and was printed and bound by The Banta Company. The cover was printed by Phoenix Color Corp.

© 2000 by Prentice-Hall, Inc.
Pearson Education
Upper Saddle River, New Jersey 07458

Printed in the United States of America

10 9 8 7 6 5 4 3 2 1

ISBN 0-13-914029-8

Prentice-Hall International (UK) Limited, *London*
Prentice-Hall of Australia Pty. Limited, *Sydney*
Prentice-Hall of Canada, Inc., *Toronto*
Prentice-Hall Hispanoamericana, S. A., *Mexico*
Prentice-Hall of India Private Limited, *New Delhi*
Prentice-Hall of Japan, Inc., *Tokyo*
Prentice-Hall (Singapore) Pte. Ltd., *Singapore*
Editora Prentice-Hall do Brasil, Ltda., *Rio de Janeiro*

For my godfather, Raymond Garber,
who was the first person to
encourage me to write.

PREFACE

This text is accompanied by the PipeSizer version 1.0 and the Sani-Sizer version 1.0. Appendix F of this text specifically addresses these two programs, which have been written in *BASIC (Beginners All-purpose System Instruction Code)* programming language. The reader should feel free to copy, study, and make changes to the programs provided on the program diskette. The PipeSizer and SaniSizer programs are designed as training tools to assist students, trainees, and others in the appropriate procedure used when planning and designing plumbing systems for commercial use.

This workbook has been divided into two parts as listed below.

PART I — BASIC PRINCIPLES

In Part I the standard design procedure is discussed. All formulas and procedures are investigated and a series of sample problems is provided. The *first* sample problem in each series is always solved completely in the text. The *second* sample problem in each series is a guided practice problem in which the reader receives hints and parts of the procedures. The last problem in each series must be completed by the reader without guidance or hints. The answers to these problems are found at the end of Part I.

A new feature in this text is the addition of topical questions. These questions appear at the end of each section for which sample problems are not needed. Unlike the material found in Volumes I and II of this workbook series, much of the material in this text does not require mathematical calculations. Therefore, sample problems do not apply to these topics. Following the discussion of such topics, a series of three topical questions has been provided. These topical questions are designed to challenge the student and, therefore, sometimes extend beyond the scope of the material discussed in the text. The answers to these questions are also found at the end of Part I.

PART II — APPLICATION PROBLEMS

This part of the workbook contains multiple word problems that mirror real-life scenarios. These problems will also include variations that may not have been discussed previously within the workbook. The answers to the problems, accompanied by detailed explanations when necessary, may be found in the answer key at the end of Part II.

ACKNOWLEDGMENTS

ASSISTANT TO THE AUTHOR
Tracy Burton

GRAPHIC ARTIST
Sabrina Johnson

PROOFREADING
Tracy Burton

TECHNICAL SUPPORT
Jennifer Bailor
Bill Dann, P.E.
Bob Karnes
Bob Kuhnert
Jeff Lyter
Bob Sites
Ellis L. Squires

REVIEWERS
D. Perry Achor, Purdue University
Marcel Sammut, architect and structural engineer
Ralph Wells, Cincinnati State Technical and Community College

CONTENTS

BUILDING SYSTEMS DESIGN SERIES

Volume III: Domestic Plumbing Design

Introduction to Plumbing

Since the days of the ancient Egyptians seeking to bring water from the far-off Nile River to the arid region of the desert, since the construction of the mighty aqueducts in Italy that were used to bring water from various rivers into areas for fertilizing land and for supplying households with potable water, humankind has sought to find the most efficient means of transporting water. This brought about the process known as **plumbing**. Plumbing simply defined is the process of using pipes to supply and remove liquid materials.

Likewise, humankind found that it was very inconvenient to store waste material and found that if there were some means to flush that material out and store it safely away from cities or inhabited areas, things would be a lot better. This brought about the process of designing sanitary waste systems, although some of the earlier attempts, especially in the Middle East (some of which can still be seen today), were not exactly sanitary.

Some early plumbing included simply digging a ditch that sloped down away from homes. These ditches were open and had no covering. They ran along city streets and by other houses and establishments. You can probably imagine what odors they might have carried with them.

Fortunately, today's plumbing systems are regulated by building codes and plumbing codes. The most common code used today is the International Plumbing Code. Plumbing codes provide rules and regulations for planning, installing, and maintaining plumbing systems.

Unlike the earlier plumbing systems, which mainly used gravity as their driving force by directing water from a reservoir downhill to a town or field, our modern plumbing systems use mechanical processes to regulate flow. Devices such as pumps are used to increase the pressure of the water. Valving can be used to decrease or regulate the pressure of the water. Complex series of electronic controls and gauges can measure water pressure, temperature, and quality for potable water and sterile water.

People discovered early on, as they realized that they needed water in areas where it was not naturally provided, that transportation of that water could sometimes be quite difficult. Sometimes the water would simply flow downhill from a higher region into a lower region and that was the ideal situation. But more often than not the water needed to be delivered to a location higher than its source. A number of different kinds of pumping mechanisms were devised, including those that worked off of windmills or horse-driven gears that would scoop water up from a river or reservoir and dump it into a pipe or channeled system. Even the force of the water itself was sometimes used. For example, the force of freshwater rushing down a river would be used to drive it back up a channel to a higher elevation. The same force might also be used to turn a large wheel that had paddles and scoops on it to scoop up the water and raise it to a higher elevation. It could then run back down and serve the areas that needed to be provided with water.

Dealing with waste material, however, was a different matter. Originally, waste material was simply scooped up manually, put into carts, carried away from a town, and buried. This worked well when the towns were very small. However, as they began to get crowded more efficient ways were needed to remove the waste. Open channels were used, some of which are still in existence in southern Asia today. The problems with open channels are obvious. In this type of system waste material simply flows, open to the air, in a channel that slopes downward away from developments. All the waste flows to a reservoir where it is gathered together to be buried or treated. Eventually we discovered that it was better to channel waste products away through a closed pipe. Some earlier forms of pipe included concrete and clay.

Initially, these concepts seemed to be ideal because the waste material had offensive odors and other unsanitary properties. By using waste pipe, the material was kept away from human contact and out of human sight. However, one of the problems that occurred included clogged pipes and the difficulty associated with cleaning those pipes. Another problem was that of siphonage. Sometimes air pockets of low pressure would form inside these enclosed pipes, causing the sewage to suck backward and come back up where it was supposed to go down. Also, when the sewage reached its final destination, it would emit offensive odors. This condition presented the problem of how to treat the sewage so that it would decompose in a timely fashion and not continue to emit offensive odors or be a health hazard.

Today our sanitary systems are very complex, and we have sewage pumping and treatment plants located throughout the United States, which are used to decompose the waste material and dispose of it in a hygienic and ecologically friendly manner.

Of course, with the advent of the industrial age, piped systems weren't simply limited to what we now call domestic water supply systems, which supply potable water. Nor were they limited to sanitary waste systems, which remove waste. Piped systems are also used to remove gases from the ground, to supply gas to homes and businesses, and to transport lubricants. Industrial application piped systems are also used to deliver steam for heating, to deliver water under high pressure for cleaning by pressure wash, and to deliver dry materials. It's not uncommon for cereals and grains to be transported from one location to another within a factory through an enclosed stainless steel pipe.

Stainless steel is also used in the transportation of organic materials because it doesn't chemically react with those materials, and it remains very sanitary. It is not uncommon for spring water, fruit juices, milk, cereals, and grains to be transported through these stainless steel pipes. Additionally, stainless steel pipes are also easy to clean.

The most common piping materials for the delivery of potable water are copper and black steel. Recently a special plastic has been introduced to the domestic water plumbing industry. It is a grayish-colored flexible plastic called polybutylene. Tubes made of these three kinds of materials are used to transport most of the drinking water and bathing water that we use from day to day. These materials are used because they are not highly reactive with water and because they don't easily combine with the materials or minerals that might be found in the water. Of these three materials copper is the most susceptible to damage from water that contains calcium carbonate. This is also known as "hard" water and sometimes does react with copper, causing the copper to break down. This is why, in many household applications, copper is being phased out and polybutylene is being used more extensively.

In sanitary waste pipes the most common material used is still iron. Cast iron is the cheapest because it requires the least amount of forming and processing before it is ready for use and it has very coarse interior and exterior surfaces. Plastics have also been introduced into the sanitary plumbing industry. One plastic that has been introduced and has been used very widely is **PVC,** which stands for polyvinyl chloride. Plastics are becoming more and more prominent in the plumbing industry. PVC is not a soft malleable plastic, but a very hard, brittle plastic that has very high tensile and shear strengths.

Today we use pipes for many different applications and, although this text focuses on domestic water piping and sanitary waste and vent piping, it's good to recognize that piping is not limited to these applications. In fact, applications of piped systems are likely to continue to grow well into the future.

PART I

Basic Principles

In Part I of this workbook, we will investigate the following topics related to commercial plumbing design:

1. Elements of a plumbing system
   a. Pipes
   b. Valves
   c. Fittings
   d. Fixtures

2. Domestic water systems
   a. Building inlet supply and regulation systems
   b. Cold water supply design and applications
   c. Hot water heating systems
   d. Hot water supply design and applications
   e. Sizing domestic water supply piping
   f. Hot water recirculation systems
   g. Domestic water plumbing plans
   h. Domestic water riser diagrams
   i. Miscellaneous considerations
      i. Pipe insulation
      ii. Hangers, anchors, riser clamps, and pipe guides
      iii. Additional methods of pipe mounting

3. Sanitary waste and vent systems
   a. Sanitary waste system design and applications
   b. Sizing sanitary waste piping

  c. Sanitary waste vent system design and applications
  d. Sizing sanitary waste vent piping
  e. Sanitary waste and vent plumbing plans
  f. Sanitary waste and vent riser diagrams

Section 1

Elements
of a Plumbing System

Plumbing is the process of using a network of pipes to distribute fluids, semisolids, or gases throughout a system. The same process may also be used to collect and remove similar waste materials from a system. In this text we will study the plumbing systems used to distribute domestic water (used for drinking and washing) and systems used to remove human waste (sanitary waste and vent systems).

Many elements make up a plumbing system. Each of these elements can be classified under one of the four following headings:

1. Pipes—used to direct substance flow

2. Valves—used to control or regulate substance flow

3. Fittings—used to connect segments of pipe

4. Fixtures—utilize the substance supplied to system

In this section we will examine each of these components in greater detail so that we can better understand the role that each one plays in a commercial plumbing system.

PIPES

We can think of **pipes** as the roadways through which a fluid may pass in order to reach its destination. Most pipes are nothing more that straight tubes, although some tubing is made of bent pipes for specific applications. For the purpose of this text, however, we will consider all pipes to be straight.

Pipes are made of a number of materials, and each material is used for a specific application or group of applications. Some of the more common pipe materials and their applications are listed in Table 1.1.

TABLE 1.1   COMMON PIPING MATERIALS USED IN COMMERCIAL PLUMBING

MATERIAL	USE(S)
Copper	Domestic water, hot water recirculation, HVAC piping
Iron	Sanitary waste, storm water
Polybutylene	Domestic water connections to fixtures
Polyvinyl chloride (PVC)	Limited sanitary waste, soil vent, storm drain, condensate piping
Steel (black)	Domestic water, HVAC piping, gas, liquid petroleum, oil

Pipes are attached to one another (as well as to valves, fittings, and fixtures) in a variety of ways. Figure 1.1 shows several kinds of pipe connections. A brief explanation of each of these connections is listed below:

Threaded — Pipes have threaded ends that resemble the outside of a screw. Fittings and couplings are screwed onto the threaded pipe ends. Threaded pipe and fittings may be specified as listed in Table 1.2.

Sweat/solder joint — A soft metal alloy of tin and lead (*solder*) with a low melting point is heated and applied to the pipe joints. When the solder cools, the joint is sealed.

FIGURE 1.1
Couplings.

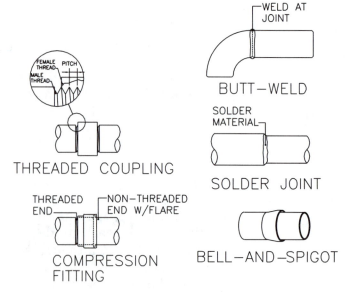

TABLE 1.2   THREADED PIPE SPECIFICATIONS

SPECIFICATION	DEFINITION
NPT	National pipe thread. Standard threading for plumbing pipe, valves, fittings, and connections in the U.S.
MPT	Male pipe thread. Denotes threading on the outside of the pipe or connection.
FPT	Female pipe thread. Denotes threading on the inside of the pipe or connection.
T.P.I.	Threads per inch. Indicates the number of threads that can be counted along a 1-inch length of threaded pipe. A pipe noted 8 T.P.I. or 8-pitch has eight threads in 1 inch.
Pitch	Distance between threads. An 8 T.P.I. or 8-pitch pipe has a thread pitch of ⅛ in.

Butt-weld — Pipe ends are beveled, then welded together using a weld bead that fills the space between the two adjoining bevels.

Hub or socket joint — An interference fit application in which the end of one pipe fits into the end of another pipe. Socket joints may or may not need additional sealing depending upon the size and application of the pipe. This fit application is also referred to as bell-and-spigot.

Compression joint — The end of one pipe is *flared* or built up to a larger diameter than the pipe itself. Then a *compression fitting* is slipped over the flared end of the pipe. This fitting is threaded at the other end and screws onto another threaded pipe end. As the fitting is tightened, it *compresses* the pipe with the flared end to the end of the threaded pipe.

TOPICAL QUESTIONS

Answer the following questions to the best of your ability based on the material covered in this portion of the text. Then check your answers with those found at the end of Part I.

1. Briefly describe the purpose of pipes in plumbing.

2. Name the method of pipe connection that you think would be appropriate for the following conditions:
   a. household copper pipe
   b. commercial black steel pipe under 2 inches
   c. large industrial stainless steel pipe

3. Where do you think that bell-and-spigot piping is used most fre-
    quently?

VALVES

Valves are used to regulate the flow of a fluid through a pipe. They
accomplish this by performing in one of the following four capacities:

Start/Stop Flow

Some of the valves that operate under this capacity, such as the **ball
valve** or the **gate valve** (shown in Figures 1.2 and 1.3), are designed
to be fully open (also called *throttle* position) or fully closed. This kind
of valve is not designed to adjust the volume or rate of flow of a fluid.
Still, other valves in this category, such as the **globe valve**, may be
used to stop fluid flow or to adjust the amount of fluid that passes
through the pipe.

Prevent Backflow

This kind of valve allows a substance to flow in a single direction
through a pipe, but prevents its flowing in the opposite direction. The
most common backflow preventing valve, shown in Figure 1.4, is the
check valve. This valve will allow a fluid to flow freely in one direction, but closes automatically when the fluid tries to flow in the opposite direction.

FIGURE 1.2
Ball valve.

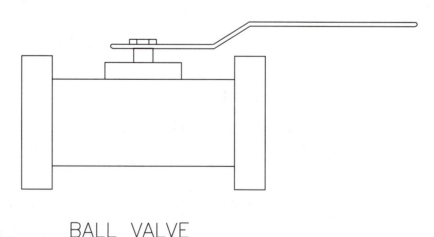

BALL VALVE

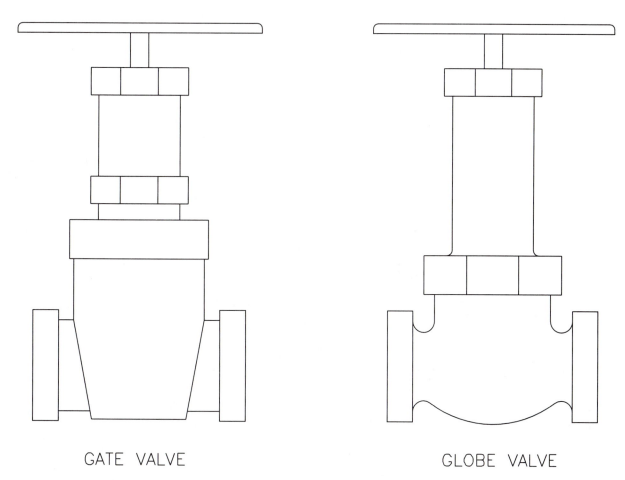

GATE VALVE   GLOBE VALVE

FIGURE 1.3
Gate and globe valves.

Reduce Pressure

Valves reduce pressure mainly in one of two ways. They either partially restrict fluid flow (such as a faucet valve or spigot), or they provide resistance to fluid flow, which creates friction. These two concepts are illustrated in Figure 1.5.

A **pressure reducing valve** is specifically designed to lower in-line fluid pressure. Its main purpose is to reduce a fluid entering a system to a lower pressure so that the fluid can be safely delivered to the system. This valve is commonly used in a valve-fitting combination known as a **pressure reducing station (PRS)**. We study this combination in depth in the Section "Building Inlet Supply and Regulation Systems." Other valves, such as the *globe valve,* may also be used to reduce fluid pressure because they restrict fluid flow and cause friction.

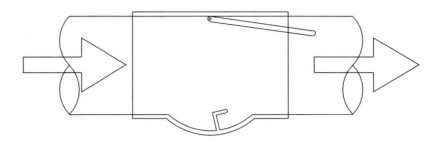

CHECK VALVE ALLOWS WATER FLOW IN PROPER DIRECTION

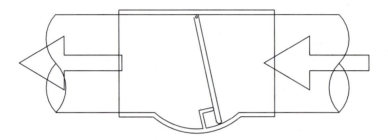

CHECK VALVE PREVENTS WATER FLOW IN IMPROPER DIRECTION

FIGURE 1.4
Operation of a swing check valve.

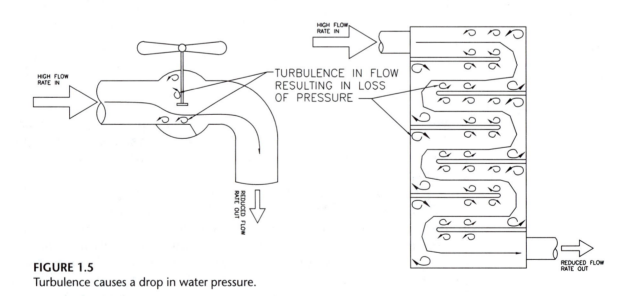

FIGURE 1.5
Turbulence causes a drop in water pressure.

FIGURE 1.6
Operation of a pressure
relief valve.

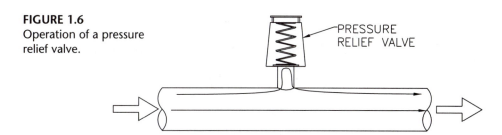

LINE PRESSURE BELOW RELIEF VALVE SETTING.
VALVE REMAINS CLOSED.

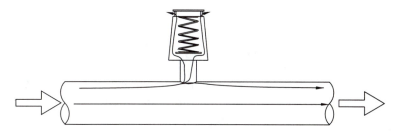

LINE PRESSURE ABOVE RELIEF VALVE SETTING.
VALVE OPENS TO RELIEVE PRESSURE.

Relieve Pressure

The valve used for this purpose is called a **pressure relief valve**, and
it is located in places that may experience sudden increases in pressure. A common location for a *pressure relief valve* in a commercial
building would be a boiler or hot water heater. When the steam or hot
air inside these units creates a certain increase in pressure, the relief
valve will open and allow some of the air/water mixture or steam to
escape. Once the pressure has dropped below the setting of the valve,
the valve will close again (see Figure 1.6).

TOPICAL QUESTIONS

Answer the following questions to the best of your ability based on the
material covered in this portion of the text. Then check your answers
with those found at the end of Part I.

1. What would you say is the primary purpose of valving?

2. Try to name at least one application for each of the following types of valves:
   a. gate valve
   b. check valve
   c. pressure reducing valve
   d. pressure relief valve

3. What do you think is the purpose of a pressure reducing station?

FITTINGS

The primary purpose of a pipe **fitting** is to join a segment of pipe to another segment of pipe. A fitting will do this in one of the three following ways:

1. Lengthening the pipe run

2. Changing the size (diameter) of the pipe run

3. Changing the direction of the pipe run

The following fittings are commonly used to attach two segments of pipe without changing the direction or size of the pipe (see Figure 1.7):

Couplings — These are short segments of pipe with threading inside each end that are used to connect two lengths of pipe together.

Unions — These fittings are used to attach piping to valves or plumbing equipment that may need to be replaced or repaired in the future. The ends of a union may be welded, bolted, or threaded onto the piping or other connections. A union is threaded in the middle and separates into two parts when loosened.

Flanges—These are pipe ends that have a circular rim that can be bolted to another *flanged* pipe, valve, or fitting. Flanges are primarily used for applications in which the fluid pressure inside the piping may be high.

The following fittings may be used to change the size of a pipe run (see Figure 1.8):

Concentric reducer — The word *concentric* means "having the same center." The purpose of any **reducer** is to change the size of the pipe. A concentric reducer is shaped like a cone with the apex (top)

FIGURE 1.7
Pipe connections.

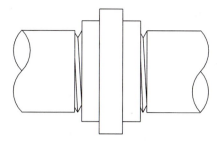

THREADED UNION

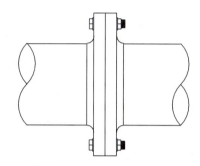

BOLTED WELD—NECK FLANGE

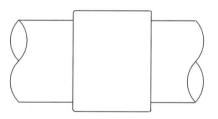

PIPE COUPLING

cut off. When two pipes of different diameters are connected using this kind of reducer, they continue to share the same center line.

Eccentric reducer — Like the concentric reducer, this reducer is also used to connect two pipes of differing sizes. However, the term *eccentric* means "having different centers." Two pipes connected with an eccentric reducer will share a common edge, but will not have the same center line.

Bushing — A pipe-end connection that has a number of applications. Bushings may be used to change the size of a pipe, connect a male-threaded pipe to a female-threaded fitting, or connect different kinds of pipe.

Adapter — This fitting is used to attach a pipe to a connection having a different size, thread pitch, or material composition.

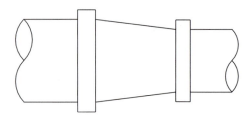

CONCENTRIC REDUCER

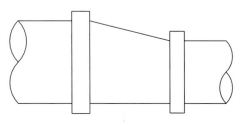

ECCENTRIC REDUCER

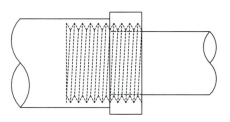

REDUCING BUSHING

These fittings are commonly used to change the direction of a pipe run or to branch out from an existing pipe run (see Figure 1.9):

Elbow — When a straight run of pipe must change direction, an elbow is used. Elbows are commonly used to connect two pipes at an angle of 22½°, 45°, or 90°. A 180° elbow, also known as a *U-bend,* may also be used. *Standard* or *short-radius* elbows have a centerline radius equal to the nominal diameter of the pipe. *Long-radius* elbows have a centerline radius equal to 1½ times the nominal pipe diameter. A *street elbow* has one male end and one female end.

Tee — A tee is used to branch out from an existing pipe run at a right angle. *Standard tees* are the same size at all three ends.

Cross — A *cross* is used to join two pipe runs at right angles when the two runs are at cross paths. Standard crosses have four connections with each having the same diameter.

FIGURE 1.9
Standard fittings.

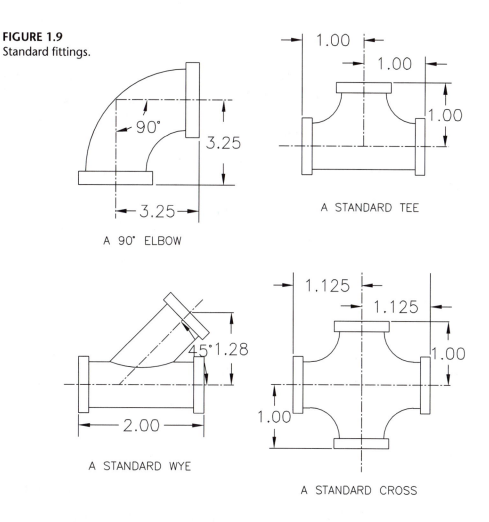

A 90° ELBOW

A STANDARD TEE

A STANDARD WYE

A STANDARD CROSS

Wye — Wyes are used in drainpipe applications. As the name implies, this fitting is shaped like the letter Y. The branch side of the wye is attached to the main side at a 45° angle so that drainage will flow smoothly from the branch into the main. A standard wye has three ends with the same diameter.

The fittings listed below are used to change the size of a pipe run while changing the direction of the pipe or branching out from a pipe (see Figure 1.10):

Elbow (reducing) — A *reducing elbow* serves the same purpose as a standard elbow except that one end of the elbow is smaller than the other end.

Tee (reducing) — *Reducing tees* commonly have a branch diameter that is smaller than the main diameter. Some reducing tees, however, have the two different main diameters or all three ends with different diameters.

Cross (reducing) — A *reducing cross* may have any combination of sizes on each of its four ends. Commonly, opposite ends have the same diameter, but this is not always the case.

Wye (reducing) — Like the reducing tee, a *reducing wye* commonly has a smaller branch connected to a larger main. However, some reducing wyes have a reduction along their mains.

Thread-o-let — This fitting is literally a threaded outlet that is cut into a pipe with a pipe tap that is placed at a right angle to the pipe run, and it acts like a pipe tee. A thread-o-let allows a threaded connection to be attached directly to a pipe where no con-

FIGURE 1.10
Reducing fittings.

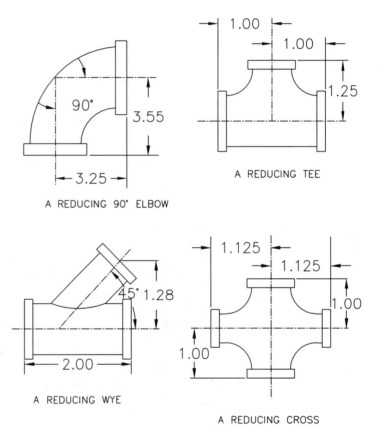

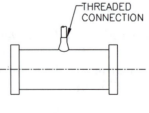

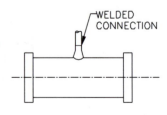

nection existed before. Thread-o-lets are always smaller than the pipe diameter.

Weld-o-let — Similar to a thread-o-let, this fitting is literally a welded outlet that is cut into a pipe with a torch or cutting tool that is placed at a right angle to the pipe run. This fitting also acts like a pipe tee. A weld-o-let allows a welded connection to be attached directly to a pipe where no connection existed before. Weld-o-lets are always smaller than the pipe diameter.

A list of fittings along with the common catalog designation for each is shown in Table 1.3.

TABLE 1.3 COMMON CATALOG DESIGNATIONS FOR PIPE FITTINGS

Fitting	Abbrv.	Particulars	Example	Meaning
reducer	red.	• May be concentric (conc.) or eccentric (ecc.) • End sizes noted by size 1 x size 2	3×2 conc. red.	Concentric reducer with one 3-in. dia. end and one 2-in. dia. end
elbow	el.	• Angle of turn • Short radius (sr) or Long radius (lr) • Street elbow (st.) • Note if reducing (red.) • Pipe diameter	1" sr 90 el. 2×1 lr 45 red. el.	1-in. dia. short-radius 90° elbow Long-radius reducing elbow with one 2-in. dia. end and one 1-in. dia. end
tee	tee	• First number indicates upstream size of main • Second number indicates downstream size of main • Third number indicates size of branch	2×2×2 tee 4×3×1 tee	Standard 2-in. tee tee with a 4-in. dia. main inlet (upstream), a 3-in. dia. main outlet (downstream), and a 1-in. dia. branch
cross	cr.	• First number indicates upstream size of main • Second number indicates downstream size of main • Third and fourth numbers indicate size of branches	4×4×4×4 cr. 2×2×1×1 cr. 3×2×½×¾	Standard 4-in. cross cross with a 2-in. dia. main and two 1-in. dia. branches cross with a main reducing from a 3-in. dia. to a 2-in. dia. and one ½-in. dia. branch and one ¾-in. dia. branch
wye	wye	Same as a tee	8×8×8 wye 6×6×4 wye	Standard 8-in. wye Wye with a 6-in. dia. main and a 4-in. dia. branch

Notes: 1. Add the word "weld," "thread," "sweat," or "socket" to indicate type of connection for fitting.
2. Include the fitting material in the designation (brass, copper, iron, steel, etc.).

Fittings are represented on plumbing floor plans in a number of ways. Figure 1.11 shows a variety of fittings in both plan and elevation views as they would be represented on a plumbing plan. On a

FIGURE 1.11
Single-line piping
examples.

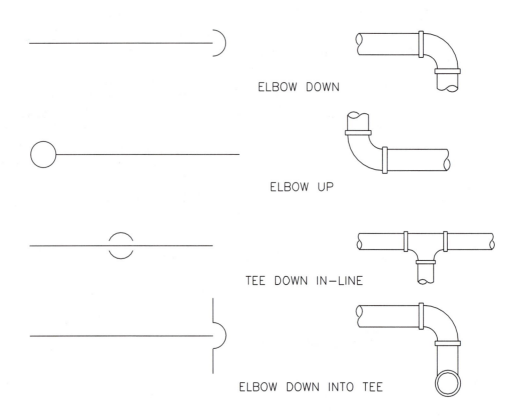

ELBOW DOWN

ELBOW UP

TEE DOWN IN—LINE

ELBOW DOWN INTO TEE

plumbing plan all piping is shown with a single line (discussed in more detail in the section "Domestic Water Plumbing Plans"). Fittings appear as circles, rectangles, or special symbols. Fittings that change the pipe direction will appear as closed or open circles. A closed circle represents a pipe that extends to the next floor or level above the one shown. A broken circle represents a pipe going down with the open side or sides of the circle being at the higher elevation(s).

When a drawing note indicates a pipe going up or down, it simply indicates the direction that the pipe is extending from the current location. This does not show the direction of flow within the pipe. Flow direction is discussed in the sections "Domestic Water Systems" and "Sanitary Waste and Vent Systems."

TOPICAL QUESTIONS

Answer the following questions to the best of your ability based on the material covered in this portion of the text. Then check your answers with those found at the end of Part I.

1. What are the three applications of pipe fittings?

2. Name two fittings for each application you listed in question 1.

3. What are three fittings that allow pipes to be connected at right angles to one another?

FIXTURES

A plumbing **fixture** is a device that utilizes the water delivered by the domestic water supply system. Fixtures may be used simply to deliver water to a location, or they may deliver water and remove waste. In this section we take a brief look at some of the more common plumbing fixtures used in a commercial building.

Lavatory (sink) — A common bathroom or rest room sink, shown in Figure 1.12, used for hand washing. Lavatories receive both hot and cold domestic water supplies. Lavatory sinks may be wall mounted or pedestal mounted.

Water closet — Commonly called a toilet or commode. Water closets may be wall or floor mounted. They operate either as *flush tank* or *flush valve* fixtures.

A **flush tank** water closet (shown in Figure 1.13) is so named because of the tank that holds water located behind the commode bowl. This kind of fixture relies on gravity and the weight of the water stored in the tank to *evacuate* (flush). When the flush lever is depressed the water in the tank empties into the bowl. This causes the contents of the bowl to empty through the drain. Meanwhile, a small valve allows a supply of cold water to refill the flush tank. A float inside the tank closes the inlet valve when the water in the tank reaches the appropriate level.

FIGURE 1.12
Lavatory sink.

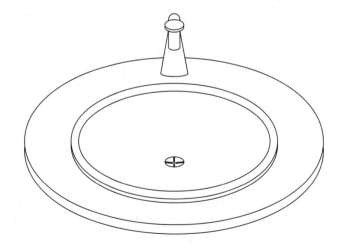

A LAVATORY SINK

FIGURE 1.13
Flush tank water closet.

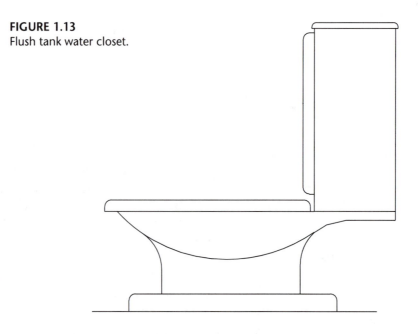

A FLUSH TANK WATER CLOSET

Flush valve fixtures rely on existing water pressure in the supply line to cause evacuation, as shown in Figure 1.14. A flush valve water closet discharges water under pressure into the commode bowl when a lever or button is depressed. This kind of fixture has no tank, but the valve must be accompanied by a device known as a **vacuum breaker**. This device is designed to prevent *siphonage,* which can cause water and other particles to be sucked into the supply line in the wrong direction (see the discussion in a later section of the Bernoulli principle and Venturi effect).

Water closets may be floor mounted or wall mounted.

Urinal — A fixture used in men's rest rooms that is designed specifically for the collection and removal of urine. Most modern urinals are the *flush valve* type; however, some varieties of antique flush tank urinals are finding their way back into some modern catalogs (see Figure 1.15).

Urinals may be wall mounted, floor mounted, pedestal type, or trough type. When used in large assembly structures, such as an arena or stadium, they are often made of stainless steel instead of the traditional porcelain of most rest room fixtures.

Service sink — Commonly made of stainless steel, this sink is used in such applications as dishwashing and rinsing. A service sink, such as the one shown in Figure 1.16, may receive hot water at a higher-than-standard temperature for the purpose of scouring and sanitizing utensils.

FIGURE 1.14
Flush valve water closet.

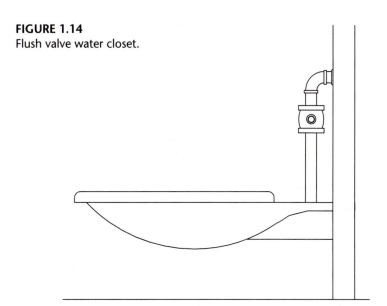

A FLUSH VALVE WATER CLOSET

FIGURE 1.15
Urinal.

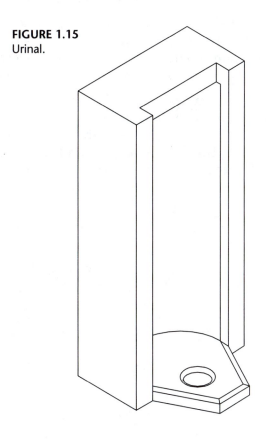

URINAL

FIGURE 1.16
Service sink.

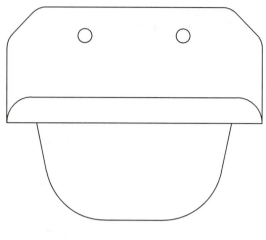

SERVICE SINK

Mop sink — This fixture, shown in Figure 1.17, is a sink mounted at floor level, sometimes placed in the corner of a janitor's closet, that is used to clean and rinse floor mops. Unlike lavatory or service sinks, mop sinks may receive only one water line.

Drinking fountain — This is a fixture that is supplied by cold water only, and its purpose is to deliver drinking water (see Figure 1.18). A drinking fountain delivers water that it receives without any further cooling. This fixture may be wall or floor mounted.

Water cooler — Similar to a drinking fountain with the exception that a water cooler contains a refrigeration unit that chills the drinking water to a set temperature (usually about 40°F). Shown in Figure 1.19, this fixture may be wall or floor mounted and must be located near an electrical power source or outlet.

FIGURE 1.17
Mop sink.

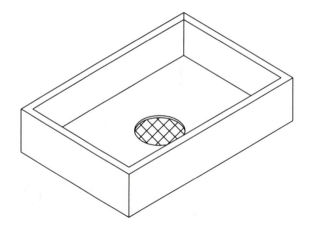

MOP SINK

FIGURE 1.18
Drinking fountain.

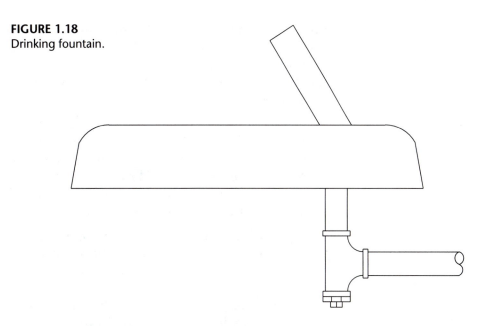

DRINKING FOUNTAIN

FIGURE 1.19
Water cooler.

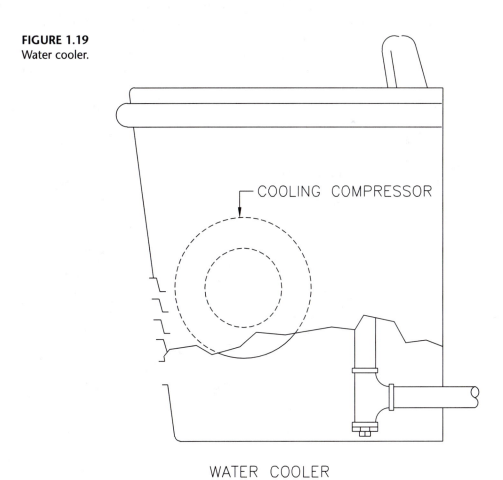

COOLING COMPRESSOR

WATER COOLER

Tub — A tub is a fixture that is designed to receive hot and cold water supplies for the purpose of bathing. A tub is most commonly used for human bathing; however, it may also have other uses such as bathing animals or soaking clothes. Tubs are usually floor mounted but also may be wall, pedestal, or leg mounted (see Figure 1.20).

Shower — This fixture has a purpose similar to that of a tub, but does not provide a vessel for immersion. A shower receives both hot and cold water supplies. Most manufacturers also provide a variety of shower/tub combinations, shown in Figure 1.21, in which the shower and tub come as a single unit.

Emergency shower — Unlike a standard shower, this fixture is simply a fixed or adjustable showerhead located above a floor drain (see Figure 1.22). The purpose of an emergency shower is to provide a means for quick rinsing of a person's skin that may have been exposed to a toxic or harmful chemical. This kind of shower is usually supplied with only cold water. Emergency showers may be wall mounted or freestanding.

Eye wash — Like an emergency shower, this fixture is located in areas where chemicals that are harmful to the eye may exist. The purpose of an eye wash, shown in Figure 1.23, is to quickly saturate the eyes of someone who has been exposed to such a chemical. Both the eye wash and the emergency shower are usually activated by a pull chain or foot lever. An eye wash is usually supplied with only cold water.

FIGURE 1.20
Tub.

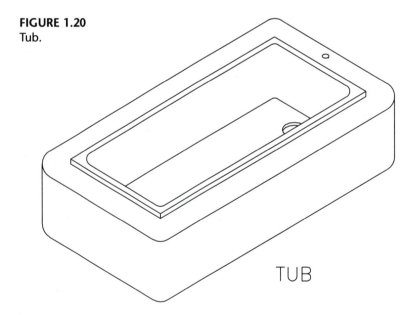

TUB

FIGURE 1.21
Shower/tub
combination.

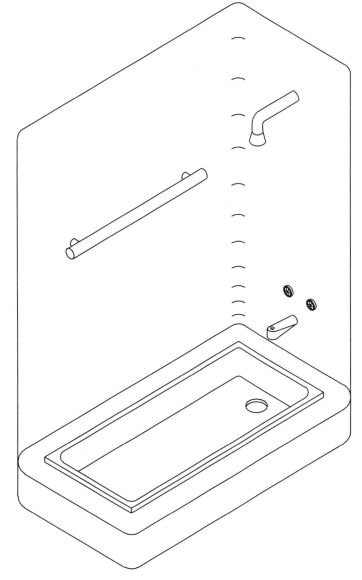

SHOWER/TUB COMBINATION

Throughout this text we examine the uses of these fixtures, as well as some others.

Hose bibb—Sometimes referred to as a water spigot or water faucet, this fixture is really a valve that is male threaded for attachment to a hose. Hose bibbs are most commonly located on the outside wall of a building (see Figure 1.24) in areas where a hose would be needed for washing down pavements or where a garden or lawn water supply might be needed. In certain locations a *secured hose bibb* may be used. This kind of hose bibb cannot be turned on without a special knob or tool that is kept in a separate location.

FIGURE 1.22
Emergency shower.

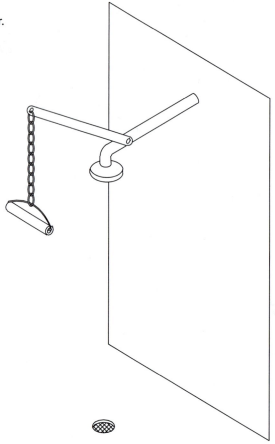

EMERGENCY SHOWER

FIGURE 1.23
Eye wash.

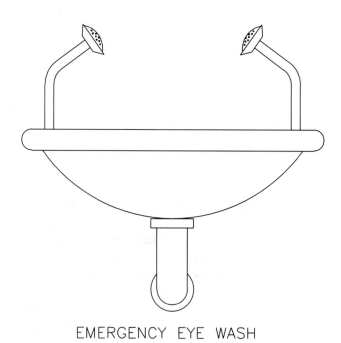

EMERGENCY EYE WASH

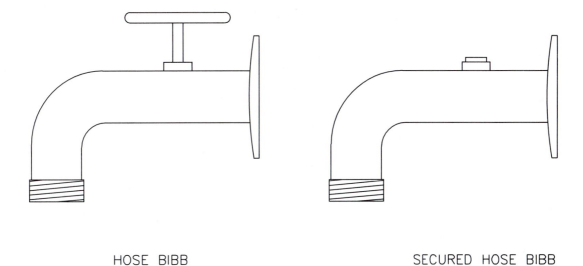

HOSE BIBB   SECURED HOSE BIBB

FIGURE 1.24
Hose bibbs.

TOPICAL QUESTIONS

Answer the following questions to the best of your ability based on the material covered in this portion of the text. Then check your answers with those found at the end of Part I.

1. Briefly define the purpose of a plumbing fixture.

2. Name three fixtures that are designed to receive only a cold water supply.

3. What is the difference between a flush valve fixture and a flush tank fixture?

SECTION 2

Domestic Water Systems

Domestic water is defined as water that is suitable for human contact and/or consumption. The domestic water system in commercial and residential applications is comprised of three distinct water systems. These systems are (1) cold water, (2) hot water, (3) hot water recirculation.

The cold water system supplies all fixtures to which it is run with domestic water at the standard water inlet temperature. Because domestic water supply lines run underground outside a building, the water in these lines will be at or near the underground temperature (approximately 55°F in most locations). Cold water lines may be insulated to prevent condensation under humid conditions, but remain otherwise unregulated for temperature control. The cold domestic water supply system is discussed in greater detail in the section "Cold Water Supply Design and Applications."

Many fixtures and appliances (such as sinks and dishwashers) require a supply of hot water. A hot water heater, supplied with water from the cold water system, is used to heat the water in this system to the desired temperature. The standard outlet temperature for a hot water heater is about 110°F to 120°F. Hot water that is needed for scouring and disinfecting is usually supplied through a separate hot water system and may reach temperatures of 140°F to 160°F. More information on this system can be found in the section "Hot Water Heating Systems."

When hot water must be delivered over a great distance (100 feet or more), it may be necessary to provide a recirculation system. This kind of domestic water system either periodically or constantly circulates water through the hot water supply system, thereby keeping the water temperature at the desired level throughout the system. We examine the principles and applications of this system in more detail in the section "Hot Water Recirculation Systems."

BUILDING INLET SUPPLY AND REGULATION SYSTEMS

Water that is used to supply a building is usually taken from a water **utility main**. This is the existing piped underground water supply that is provided by the local water utility company. A pipe is attached to the utility main and is then run to the building. When the main water supply reaches the building inlet (location at which the water line enters the building), it must go through a number of processes before it is delivered to the various building domestic water systems. These processes include, but are not always limited to, pressure regulation, filtration, purification and treatment, heating, and chilling.

Pressure Regulation

This is the adjustment of water pressure in the line for use in the building system. The three processes used to regulate water pressure are:

1. **Reducing** — The process of decreasing water pressure in the supply line to a desired level, primarily using a valve or series of valves and fittings.

2. **Increasing** — The process of raising the supply line water pressure to the level needed for service to the building, usually by means of a mechanical water pump.

3. **Balancing** — The process of maintaining water pressure at a desired level under conditions in which the supply line pressure may change suddenly or frequently.

The process of *pressure reduction* is most often accomplished by the use of a **pressure reducing station**. Figure 1.25 shows a drawing of a pressure reducing station, and a plumbing schematic of the same station. A pressure reducing station is needed only when the utility water supply pressure is too high for the building system to utilize safely.

A pressure reducing station is made of four basic assemblies and may contain one or more of each of these assemblies. These are the (1) high-pressure supply inlet, (2) pressure reducing valve, (3) automatic/manual bypass, and (4) system pressure supply outlet. Figure 1.26 shows the pressure reducing station from Figure 1.25 broken into these four assemblies.

FIGURE 1.25
Pressure reducing
station schematic.

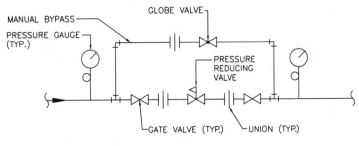

PRESSURE REDUCING STATION DETAIL
SCALE: NONE

FIGURE 1.26
Pressure reducing
station assemblies.

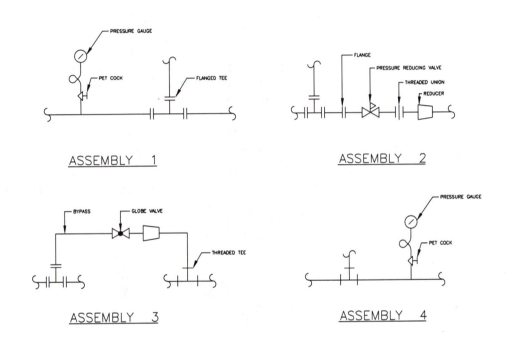

The high-pressure inlet side of the PRS (pressure reducing station) receives water directly from the utility main at a higher pressure than that which can be safely utilized by the building domestic water system. For this reason, the fittings located on the inlet side of the PRS are all *flanged*. We use flanged fittings in locations where the water pressure may be too high for threaded pipe to handle. Assembly 1 in Figure 1.26 shows a flanged tee that is used to link the bypass to the main inlet for the station.

Notice the pressure gauge located near the inlet side of the PRS. This device measures the pressure of the incoming water from the utility main. Sometimes this gauge is connected electronically to a motorized regulator on the pressure reducing valve. This type of assembly automatically adjusts the setting of the valve so that the system pressure remains constant. Other pressure reducing valves have manual adjustments that are set at the time of system start-up.

A technician will adjust the pressure reducing valve setting while reading the pressure gauge located on the outlet side of the PRS.

Most pressure reducing stations have at least one bypass in the event that the pressure reducing valve fails to function properly. The bypass is usually equipped with a valve that can be easily adjusted by hand, such as a globe valve. This bypass valve can be used to regulate the pressure of the water as it passes through the PRS until the pressure reducing valve can be repaired or replaced.

In some instances it is necessary actually to increase the water pressure in the supply line before it is distributed throughout the building for service. This may occur when water is taken from a local ground source or reservoir, or when the building is located at an elevation that is significantly higher than the water supply source. In such instances we can provide one or more pumping stations to increase the water line pressure. These pumping stations can be located within the mechanical room of the building, or they may be placed in a pump house somewhere outside the building.

Figure 1.27 shows an example of a typical single-pump pumping station for a small commercial building. Notice the concrete house-keeping pad below the pump and the flexible connections to the water line at either end of the pump. These are necessary elements because the pump is a vibrating piece of equipment. The concrete pad is used to isolate the pump from the rest of the building foundation so that the foundation does not experience weakening and cracking due to the vibration caused by the pump. The flexible pipe connections prevent the same vibrations from being transmitted along one of the pipes to the pipe support system (which could cause weakening and collapse).

Gate valves and unions have been placed on the water lines at either end of the pump so that the pump can be taken off-line and serviced if necessary. This is generally done by first closing each of the gate valves (this stops the water from flowing to the pump from each direction), then removing the threaded unions (which allows the pump

FIGURE 1.27
In-line pumping station.

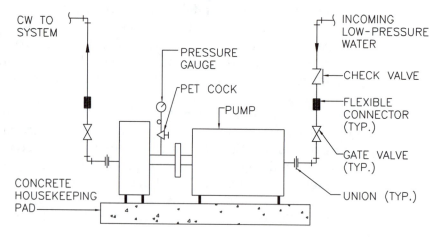

to be completely separated from the system).

Figure 1.28 shows an example of a mechanical room layout with a domestic water line pump in place. For applications in which there may be a higher risk of pump failure, or when a building simply cannot go without water for any significant period of time, the designer or engineer may recommend the installation of a backup water pump. This pump would be used in the event that the primary water supply pump either had failed or had need of being taken off-line for repair. Figure 1.29 illustrates the layout of a mechanical room that has a backup water pump and supply bypass.

Filtration

Many domestic water supply systems for commercial buildings employ the use of one or more **strainers** in the inlet supply line (see Figure 1.30) to trap any solid particles that might be suspended in the water. There are several types of in-line strainers and most of these incorporate a way to clean the strainer filter.

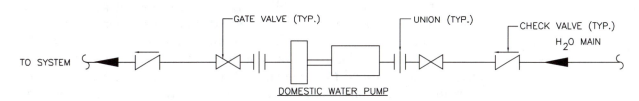

FIGURE 1.28
In-line pump schematic.

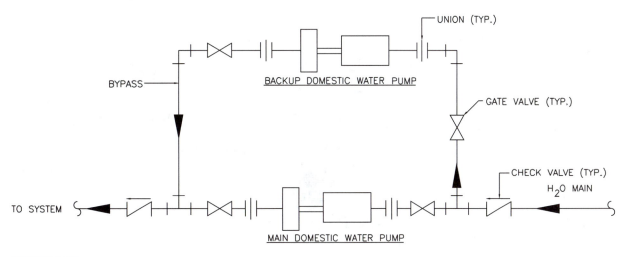

FIGURE 1.29
In-line pump with backup.

FIGURE 1.30
Strainer.

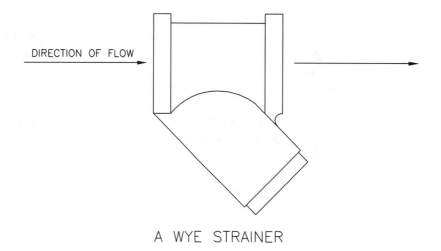

DIRECTION OF FLOW

A WYE STRAINER

One method involves the removal and cleaning or replacement of the strainer filter. Such strainers usually will be accompanied by a stop valve that prevents water from flowing through the strainer while the filter is being serviced (see Figure 1.31).

Another method of filter cleaning is by the use of a **blowdown** valve. This valve is located a few inches downstream from the strainer and is opened periodically to allow the water to flow freely through the filter, as shown in Figure 1.32. The force of the water will flush out any particles trapped in the strainer filter. Once the filter is clean, the blowdown valve is closed. When the blowdown valve is used, the strainer assembly must be connected to a flush line, or it must be located near a floor drain.

FIGURE 1.31
Exploded view of strainer.

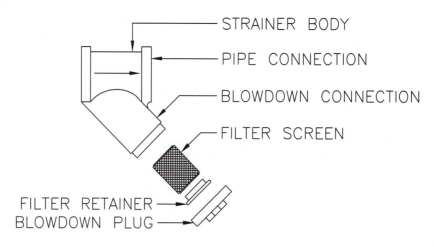

STRAINER BODY

PIPE CONNECTION

BLOWDOWN CONNECTION

FILTER SCREEN

FILTER RETAINER

BLOWDOWN PLUG

EXPLODED VIEW OF A WYE STRAINER

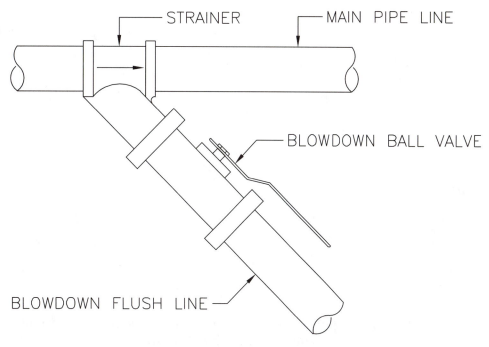

FIGURE 1.32
Strainer with blowdown
and flush line.

STRAINER — MAIN PIPE LINE

BLOWDOWN BALL VALVE

BLOWDOWN FLUSH LINE

A WYE STRAINER WITH BLOWDOWN
VALVE AND FLUSH LINE

Purification and Treatment

Water that is received from a public utility water main has already undergone numerous processes to ensure its cleanliness, purity, and palatability (ability to be ingested). Sometimes, though, it is necessary to treat the incoming water supply further before it is delivered to the building system.

One of the most common water treatment processes is that which is used for reducing the level of calcium and other minerals in the water. By adding certain **water softening** chemical salts, such as those used in the system shown in Figure 1.33, we can reduce the hardness, or mineral content, of the water. **Hard water** may have a metallic taste and may leave a greenish or bluish stain on water fixtures. This happens most noticeably in fixtures that contain water for long periods of time, such as toilets and bathtubs. Additionally, hard water can leave mineral deposits inside the pipes through which it travels. Left untreated this condition will eventually cause clogged piping and irreversible pipe damage.

Another form of water treatment involves adding certain nontoxic chemicals to the water to prevent the spread of waterborne parasites. Many of these parasites are responsible for headaches, nausea, and diarrhea. Most public water utilities are able to eliminate these parasites in the water before it is delivered into the mains for public use. However, many homes and buildings receive water that is delivered from a local groundwater source, which may not have been previously treated for parasite elimination. Water delivered from these sources

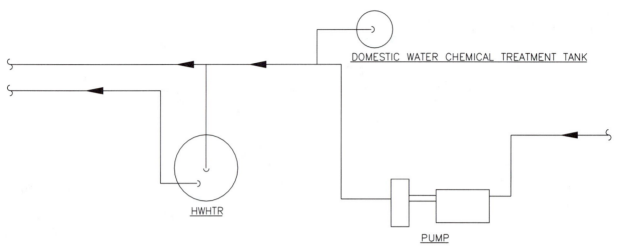

FIGURE 1.33
Hard water treatment system.

will often be treated with an iodine-based chemical solution, which kills most organisms harmful to humans.

Heating

Water that is supplied to a building has many possible uses. Some of these uses require the water to be supplied at a higher temperature. Appliances or fixtures that have these requirements will often utilize water delivered by the domestic hot water system. Sinks, showers, washtubs, and dishwashers are just a few of the many fixtures and appliances that make use of the domestic hot water system. In the section "Hot Water Heating Systems," we examine the means by which some of the water supplied to a building is heated for use by this system.

It is also important to note at this point that the water temperature in a domestic hot water system may be carefully regulated depending upon its intended use. Hot water lines are generally insulated to prevent significant loss of heat over the length of the pipe run.

Chilling

Sometimes drinking water is made cooler by a mechanical process before it reaches a drinking fountain. This process called **chilling** is usually done by a refrigeration unit. Water may be chilled by a central water **chiller** that is designed to chill large quantities of water before distribution, or the water may be chilled by a small refrigeration unit located inside a water cooler or dispenser.

Chilled water piping is usually insulated to keep the water cold and to prevent condensation (sweating) on the outside of the cold pipes.

TOPICAL QUESTIONS

Answer the following questions to the best of your ability based on the material covered in this portion of the text. Then check your answers with those found at the end of Part I.

1. Provide a complete definition for domestic water.

2. Briefly describe the pressure regulation process for an incoming domestic water supply.

3. Name two possible uses for chilled water.

COLD WATER SUPPLY DESIGN AND APPLICATIONS

When we speak of cold water in a domestic water system, we are referring to water that is neither heated nor cooled by any artificial process. The water in a domestic cold water supply system may be as cold as 40°F or as warm as 65°F. The temperature of the water in this system is completely dependent upon the path that the water has taken to reach its destination. For instance, water that arrives at a building inlet at 40°F from the underground piping, then sits in the pipes in a mechanical equipment room for 8 hours before being delivered to a sink, will not come out of the faucet feeling very cold. For this reason, we distinguish a *cold water* system from a *chilled water* system, because chilled water is maintained at a low temperature by some artificial means.

A number of plumbing fixtures receive water from the domestic cold water supply system. Among the most common of these fixtures are water closets, lavatory sinks, tubs and showers, hose bibbs, and urinals, just to name a few. The hot water heater for the domestic hot water supply system is also supplied with water from the cold water supply system. The hot water supply system is discussed in detail in the next section.

When planning a domestic water plumbing system for a commercial building, a number of factors must be taken into consideration.

First, we must look at the need for plumbing fixtures throughout the building. This is done most readily by looking at the floor plans provided by the building architect. Once we examine these plans, we can determine the best location for each fixture in each room or space. Often, the building architect will suggest these locations on the building floor plans; however, it is the responsibility of the mechanical designer or engineer in charge of the plumbing design to verify and/or adjust these locations as needed. A number of local and national building codes place strict conditions on the placement and spacing of certain domestic water plumbing fixtures. The **ADA** (Amercans with Disabilities Act) requires that all rest rooms designed for use by the general public must have at least one handicapped-accessible fixture of each type. These fixtures must meet strict minimum clearance requirements so that they are readily accessible to wheelchair-bound individuals. Figure 1.34 shows some examples of ADA-compliant public rest room fixtures.

Additionally, the mechanical designer for a plumbing system must ensure that all supply piping has a clear path from the supply main to each fixture. The designer must carefully plan the routing of each pipe, while planning for control and shutoff valving and contingencies for repair and/or replacement of faulty fixtures.

Because most pipes used in a domestic water supply system are relatively small, they usually are not a problem for the designer to locate. However, some water supply mains in larger buildings can be quite large. In fact, it is not unusual for a cold water supply main in a large building to be 8 to 10 inches in diameter. When we add an inch of insulation to a pipe this big, we can end up with a pipe that measures over a foot in diameter! So pipe size is an important consideration when the mains are supplying large amounts of water to the building.

Sometimes the architect will provide vertical openings between two adjoining rooms. These openings are called **chases** and they are specifically designed to allow adequate space for the pipes to run inside walls. A chase that is used for piping only is called a **plumbing chase**. If the chase is used for both plumbing and HVAC, then it is

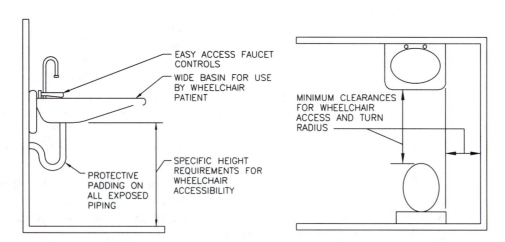

TO MEET ADA COMPLIANCE, PLUMBING FIXTURES MUST MEET
MINIMUM CLEARANCE AND SAFETY REQUIREMENTS

FIGURE 1.34
ADA compliance criteria.

referred to as a **mechanical chase**. Chases that have been located for use by all building systems (plumbing, HVAC, electrical, etc.) are called **common chases**. If the architect has not provided a chase in a location where one would be helpful (or necessary), the designer can request to have one placed in that location. It is important that the mechanical designer coordinate all chase location additions or changes with the architect because the addition of a chase will change the architecture of the adjoining rooms (wall locations, floor area, room size/shape, etc.). Figure 1.35 shows some examples of various chases.

Fixture placement is also an important factor to consider in the layout of a domestic plumbing system. Some of the factors to consider in determining the placement of fixtures are:

Convenience for accessibility and use

Ease of installation

Accessibility for maintenance

Grouping for zoning

Minimizing the use of supply piping

FIGURE 1.35
Plan views of chases.

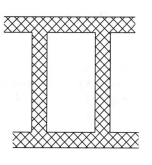

COMMON CHASE

BOX CHASE

CORNER CHASE

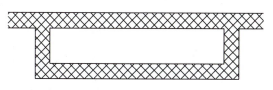

CHASE ALONG WALL

The first three items in this list are self-explanatory. The last two, however, require a brief explanation. When we speak of **zoning**, we mean that a group of fixtures is being serviced by the same water main or branch. Figure 1.36 shows a pair of rest rooms, one with all fixtures supplied directly from the water main and the other zoned with a branch off of the main. A major advantage of *zoning* water supply is that a separate shutoff valve can be placed on the zone branch. This means that if a fixture in that zone needs to be repaired water would need to be shut off only for that zone. The rest of the building would continue to receive an uninterrupted water supply.

One of the most common methods of minimizing the quantity of supply piping to be used is to place fixtures in a single room or adjoining rooms along a common wall. This allows us to deliver water to two or more fixtures at a time using only one pipe. By the way, carefully planned zoning can also result in the reduction of the quantity of pipe required to supply a group of fixtures.

Looking at Figure 1.37, we can see that two rows of plumbing fixtures placed along a common wall can be supplied with one branch of piping if a plumbing chase is built into the common wall. This is also a common method of reducing the amount of pipe required to supply a group of fixtures. In fact, with a valve placed on the inlet side of this pipe branch, we can treat this group of fixtures as a single zone.

Standard cold water plumbing pipes do not require much special attention in their design. They are sometimes insulated to prevent condensation or heat gain from warm surroundings. Also, domestic cold water supply piping is most commonly made of copper. Larger sizes (greater than 2 inches in diameter) are commonly made of black steel pipe, which is stronger than copper. There are also some plastic alloys, such as **polybutlylene**, which are sturdy, malleable (meaning they can be easily shaped), and corrosion resistant, that are used for cold water supply lines.

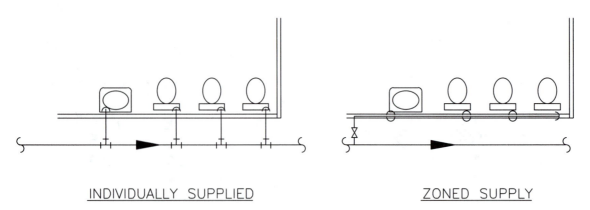

INDIVIDUALLY SUPPLIED   ZONED SUPPLY

FIGURE 1.36
Individual versus zoned supply.

FIGURE 1.37
Common wall
plumbing chase.

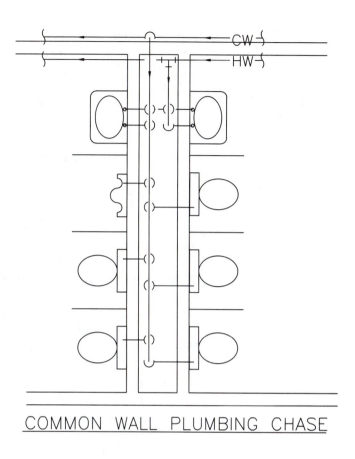

COMMON WALL PLUMBING CHASE

Designers must follow several general rules when laying out a piping system. The following several paragraphs list, in no particular
order, a number of these rules; although we discuss these rules here
they apply to both hot and cold water systems.

All piping should be run to fixtures in an ordered manner. The layout should make the most efficient use of the pipe and should incorporate the use of the most common and available fittings. As a general
rule, we should try to make all pipe turns using 45° and 90° elbows
because these are the most common and least expensive elbows. Obvi-
ously, this is not always possible, but we should make use of these
common fittings whenever we can.

We should try to run all pipe parallel to the building wall lines wherever possible. This makes the pipe easier to hang and easier to locate for
repairs after installation. Pipe runs should occur in areas that are most
easily accessed for the building. For instance, a building that has all
drop ceilings generally has water supply mains running through the ceiling above the corridors. If a plumber needs to make repairs to a piping
system designed in this manner, he or she could access the piping in the
ceiling simply by removing the necessary ceiling tiles. Vertical pipe runs
should take place in wall chases wherever possible. Some vertical pipe

drops can occur within or along the exterior of a wall, but these applications should be limited because exposed pipe is unprotected and unsightly, and pipes in wall spaces are difficult to access for repair.

Valves for supply pipes should be located where they can be readily accessed for quick adjustment. Access to shutoff valves should not be restricted or hindered in any way. Because a water leak can spread quickly, it is vitally important that a leaking supply line be closed promptly to avoid property damage and dangerous conditions for the building occupants. Valves can be located in specially designed **valve boxes**, they can be fully exposed (see Figure 1.38), they can be placed in piping chases, or they can be located in an accessible ceiling space above ceiling tiles or behind an access door. These locations should be clearly marked on all design and construction drawings and should be made available to the building maintenance personnel.

All piping in the same supply system should be made of the same material. All fittings, valves, and connections to fixtures must be made of materials that are compatible for connecting to the supply piping. When a system suddenly changes from one material to another, a few things must be considered:

1. If the connection involves two different metals, then a **dielectric fitting** is usually required. This fitting diffuses the difference in electrical potential between the two metals and retards corrosion.

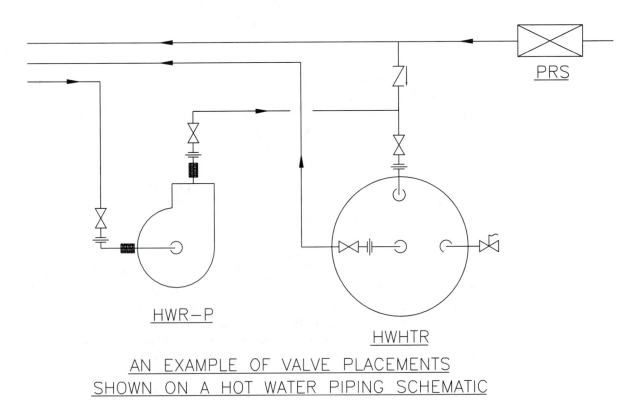

FIGURE 1.38
Valve placements.

2. If the connection involves a metal and a plastic (such as copper to PVC), then the plastic fitting must be designed to attach securely to the metal pipe without risk of damage to the plastic side of the connection.

The same method of pipe connection should occur as often as possible throughout the system. This means that a system that primarily uses threaded pipe should make use of threaded valves, fittings, and fixture connections as much as possible. The type of pipe end connections that a system should have are generally defined in the **job specifications** prepared by the mechanical engineer.

All piping in a water supply system should be run as close as possible to the same elevation throughout a zone, or throughout the entire building if possible. When we define the elevation of a pipe, we usually indicate its **invert elevation**. This is the elevation to the bottom of the insulation of an insulated pipe or to the bottom of an uninsulated pipe. The abbreviation *inv.* following a dimension on a drawing means that the elevation is an *invert*. We will discuss pipe elevation notation more thoroughly in the section "Hangers, Anchors, Riser Clamps, and Pipe Guides."

It is also very important that we use pipe rise and drop symbols to indicate when there is to be a change in pipe elevation. Figure 1.39 shows a number of examples of pipe elevation changes and **takeoffs** as they appear in a plan view. Also, when one pipe crosses another pipe

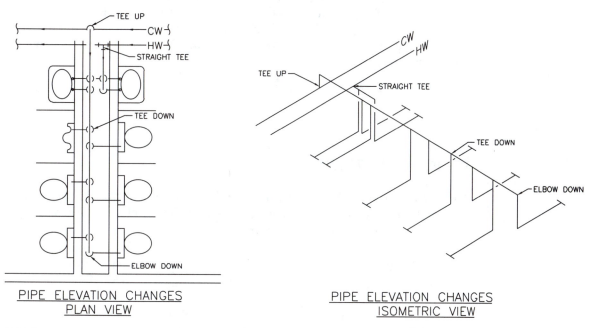

PIPE ELEVATION CHANGES
PLAN VIEW

PIPE ELEVATION CHANGES
ISOMETRIC VIEW

FIGURE 1.39
Pipe elevation changes.

they must be run at different elevations, and the pipe at the lower elevation must be broken to indicate that it is the lower pipe.

As a piping designer you should try your best to show all changes in direction and elevation of your piping on the plumbing drawings. However, it is seldom realistic to expect that a person sitting in an office looking at drawings of a building will accurately be able to account for all of the conflicts and problems that may arise during construction. For this reason you must understand that the path you select for your pipe can be considered a suggested route, but not necessarily the one that the pipe fitters will be able to use in actual installation. If you are careful to connect your systems correctly, however, this will reduce many potential problems.

The last item that we address here is that of attaching pipes of different sizes to one another. Whenever possible, the plumbing designer should provide the smallest size change available between two adjoining pipes. For example, if a 2-inch pipe needs to be connected to a smaller pipe, the next size available is a 1½-inch pipe. If the next segment of pipe is required to be only 1 inch in diameter, we might still use a 1½-inch pipe for part of the run. By gradually reducing the pipe size, we reduce the amount of turbulence created and also avoid excessive loss of pressure.

It is important to remember that every time a pipe size changes, every time a pipe turns, and every time a branch is taken off a main, the pressure in the water will drop. In each of these instances the water turbulence will also increase. Therefore, it is wise to design a piping layout that minimizes direction and size changes. Of course, in certain instances it is difficult to avoid large quantities of turns and takeoffs; however, we should be careful not to use fittings to excess.

TOPICAL QUESTIONS

Answer the following questions to the best of your ability based on the material covered in this portion of the text. Then check your answers with those found at the end of Part I.

1. Briefly explain the primary difference between a cold water supply system and a chilled water supply system.

2. What is the purpose of a chase? Name some building disciplines that might use chases.

3. What is meant by a zoned supply?

HOT WATER HEATING SYSTEMS

The *domestic hot water* system is designed to be used for drinking, cooking, washing, and sanitizing. Water in this system is heated using a **domestic hot water heater**. Although the hot water heater can be set to a variety of temperatures, it is most commonly set to temperatures of 110°F to 120°F for most domestic applications. Water over 130°F can cause a first-degree burn (similar to a sunburn) in just a few seconds. In many establishments, such as health-care facilities and hotels, the water supply to the lavatory sinks and showers is limited to a temperature of 120°F or less.

Water that is heated to a temperature of between 85°F and 120°F is called **tempered water**. **Hot water** is actually defined by the Internation Plumbing Code as water that is above 120°F. This means that most domestic hot water applications are actually using *tempered water*.

Water heated to a temperature higher than 135°F is considered to be scalding. At this temperature a burn can occur very quickly. Water over 160°F causes instant burns to skin. Prolonged exposure to water at this temperature or above can cause serious injury. Most domestic water plumbing systems restrict the use of water over 130°F to cleaning and sanitizing. This helps to prevent accidental injury to the public when using hot water from a plumbing fixture.

A cold water supply is delivered to a hot water heater, shown in Figure 1.40. The domestic hot water heater is actually just a large canister that contains a water supply and a device that is used to heat the water. Following is a list of standard components for a hot water heater:

Jacket — The outer covering of the heater body.

Body — The main element of the heater. The body contains the water, coils, heat source, and temperature controls.

Thermostat — The temperature control device. The thermostat may be located inside a panel behind the jacket, or it may be fully exposed. This device automatically regulates the temperature of the water inside the heater by turning the heating element/burner on and off as needed.

Heating element/burner — If the hot water heater is an electric model, then it will generate heat with an electric heating element. Electricity passes through a series of metal coils that get hot and heat the water inside the unit. In a gas-fired hot water heater, a gas line is attached to a pilot light inlet. When the automatic temperature control signals for more heat, a gas valve is opened, which allows a larger burner section to be filled with gas. The gas

FIGURE 1.40
Hot water heater.

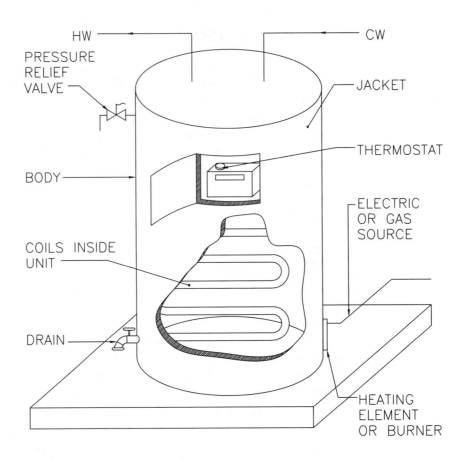

is then ignited by the pilot light and heat is generated for the water.

Pressure relief valve — This valve is a safety feature that prevents the heater from bursting due to excessive temperature and pressure. As water is heated, it expands, which creates an elevated pressure inside the heater. When the pressure exceeds the setting on the pressure relief valve, the valve opens and excess water and air are allowed to escape. When the pressure drops below the safety level the valve automatically closes again. This valve is *normally closed*.

Drain — If the unit needs to be serviced or replaced, all of the water must first be removed. The drain is usually located at the bottom of the unit and is coupled with a shutoff valve that can be opened to allow the water inside the unit to escape. This valve is *normally closed*.

A hot water heater is used to raise the temperature of some of the domestic water supply for use in various fixtures. The hot water heater tank is also used as a reservoir in which hot water can be stored and kept at temperature until it is needed by the system.

TOPICAL QUESTIONS

Answer the following questions to the best of your ability based on the material covered in this portion of the text. Then check your answers with those found at the end of Part I.

1. What is the difference between a hot water supply and a tempered water supply?

2. Name two sources of heat for a domestic hot water heater.

3. Why should a hot water heater be placed near a floor drain?

HOT WATER SUPPLY DESIGN AND APPLICATIONS

The general layout of hot water piping is very similar to that of cold water piping. There are, however, two distinct differences (other than temperature) between these two systems. First, the hot water piping must be insulated to prevent heat loss and risk of injury in exposed areas. Second, because more appliances use cold water than hot water, we generally use smaller pipes for the hot water system (discussed further in the next section).

Additional considerations must be addressed when designing a hot water system. One is the possibility of water expanding inside the pipes due to the elevated temperature, and the other is the necessity of periodically recirculating the water so that the water resting in the pipes does not get too cool. Both of these considerations are addressed in subsequent sections of this text.

Looking at Figure 1.41, we can see a sample of a domestic hot water piping layout. Notice that the hot water lines do not run to the urinal and toilets shown (of course!). Note also that these lines run to the left side of the sink and shower valve. Other than these conditions, the hot water pipe is run in the same manner as the cold water pipe.

Sometimes a hot water service is required for dishwashers, service cleaning sinks, and the like. When a hot water line is to be hotter than the regular hot water service to the building, we must label that line in the appropriate manner. Figure 1.42 shows a 130°F hot water line running from the hot water heater (HWHTR) to a dishwasher (DW) and a service sink (SS). Notice that the supply line is labeled 130°. The recirculation line (discussed later) is shown as a solid line with three broken lines.

When a system requires hot water only for standard domestic applications (lavatory sinks, showers, baths), then the water heater thermostat can be adjusted to about 120°F. As mentioned earlier, by

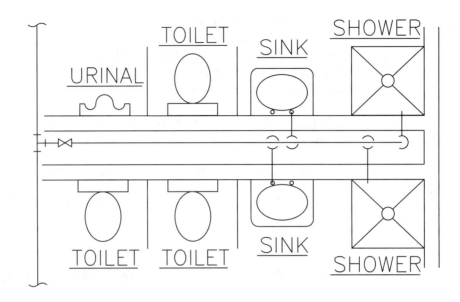

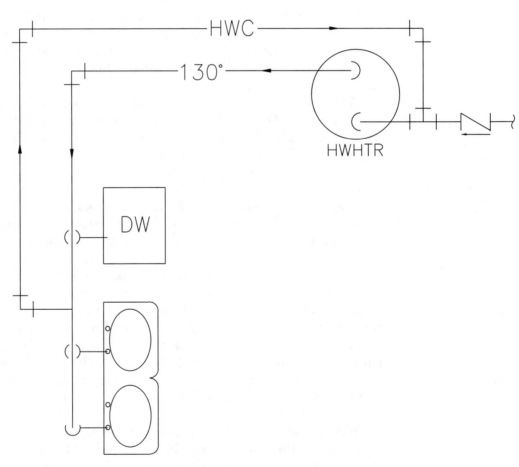

FIGURE 1.42
A 130°F hot water line.

setting the temperature to this level we can prevent scalding injuries that might be caused by water that is too hot.

If a system requires both tempered water and true hot water, we can provide these services in one of two ways. First, we can use more than one hot water heater, as shown in Figure 1.43. The advantage to this setup is that we can thermostatically control each system individually and one system will not affect the other. The primary disadvantage is cost. Two water heaters that must be installed separately, both requiring the same amount of labor, and both needing the same maintenance, create a significant additional cost.

The second method to provide both tempered and hot water to the same system is shown in Figure 1.44. All of the water is heated by a single hot water heater to the highest required temperature for the system and then is delivered to the system. The water delivered directly to the system is the hot water used for sanitation. The water to be used for hand washing, bathing, and so forth is tempered through a **mixing valve**. A mixing valve is used to adjust the temperature of the hot water by adding a metered amount of cold water to the same supply line. Mixing valves may be manually set and adjusted or they may be electronically controlled to regulate temperature. The advantage of the mixing valve is obvious: Only one hot water heater is needed to supply the system, thus reducing cost and maintenance. One disadvantage is that the entire hot water system is tied together. If the heater needs maintenance, then both systems must be shut down.

TOPICAL QUESTIONS

Answer the following questions to the best of your ability based on the material covered in this portion of the text. Then check your answers with those found at the end of Part I.

1. Why are hot water mains generally smaller than cold water mains in a building?

2. What process may be used to ensure that the hot water in a hot water supply system remains hot in pipes located far from the hot water heater?

3. What kind of valve can be used to temper a hot water supply by blending hot water with cold water?

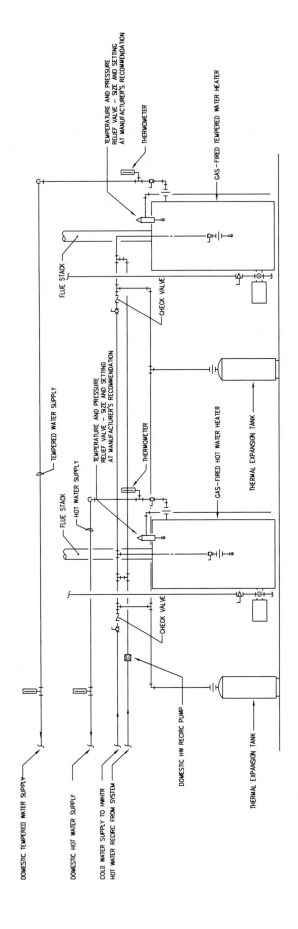

FIGURE 1.43
Tempered versus hot water supply.

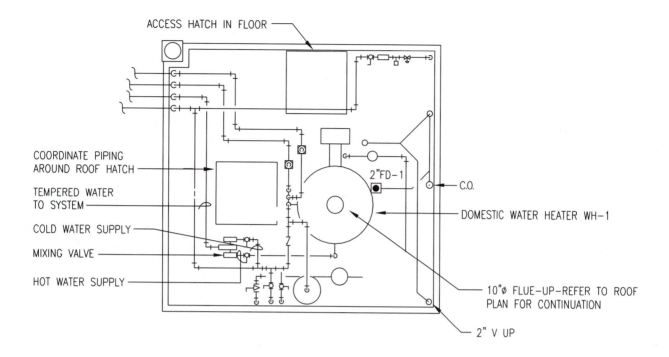

HOT WATER VERSUS TEMPERED WATER W/MIXING VALVE

FIGURE 1.44
Hot and tempered water supplies with mixing valve.

SIZING DOMESTIC WATER SUPPLY PIPING

Both hot and cold water systems are sized in the same manner. The size, or nominal diameter, of a pipe is based primarily upon the amount of water that must flow through that pipe over a given period of time. The unit of **volumetric flow**, or volume per unit time, that we most commonly use in the plumbing industry is **gallons per minute (gpm)**. The greater the water demand the larger the pipe size will need to be.

To illustrate the concept of volumetric flow in gallons per minute, let's refer to Figure 1.45. Notice that in the far left illustration the 10-gallon drum is empty. The center illustration shows the drum half full (5 gallons) after the spigot is open for 30 seconds, and in the far right illustration the drum is completely full after one minute. Because it took one full minute to fill the drum with 10 gallons of water, we say that the volumetric flow of water was 10 gpm. If we further assume that the water was flowing at a constant rate during the entire minute, then we could use the following formula to determine the flow rate at any point in time if we know the amount of water delivered in gallons, and the amount of time in minutes.

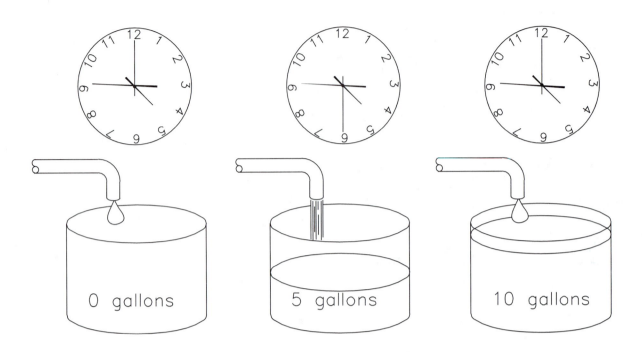

A FLOW RATE OF 10 GPM

FIGURE 1.45
Illustration of volumetric flow rate.

$$gpm = gallons\ delivered/time\ of\ delivery\ in\ minutes$$

If, for example, we held an 8-ounce glass under a kitchen faucet that is fully open, and the glass filled to the top in 2 seconds, we could find the volumetric rate of flow by:

$$gpm = volume/time$$

$$where\ volume = 8\ oz\ (1\ gal/128\ oz) = 0.0625\ gal$$
$$time\ \ \ \ = 2\ sec\ (1\ min/60\ sec) = 0.03\ min$$

$$gpm = 0.0625\ gal/(0.03\ min)$$
$$gpm = 2.08\ or\ approx.\ \mathbf{2\ gpm}$$

The unit used in plumbing design to determine the diameter of a pipe based on the amount of water it is required to deliver is called the **water supply fixture unit** (abbreviated **wsfu**). The wsfu is an arbitrary unit that indicates the amount of **demand** (required water flow) in a system. Appendix A at the end of this text is the table found in the International Plumbing Code book for estimating demand in wsfu for part or all of a plumbing system. Table 1.4 lists many of the common plumbing fixtures used in commercial building and the corresponding

TABLE 1.4   **LOAD VALUES ASSIGNED TO FIXTURES[a]**

FIXTURE	OCCUPANCY	TYPE OF SUPPLY CONTROL	LOAD VALUES, IN WATER SUPPLY FIXTURE UNITS		
			Cold	Hot	Total
Bathroom group	Private	Flush tank	2.7	1.5	3.6
Bathroom group	Private	Flush valve	6.0	3.0	8.0
Bathtub	Private	Faucet	1.0	1.0	1.4
Bathtub	Public	Faucet	3.0	3.0	4.0
Bidet	Private	Faucet	1.5	1.5	2.0
Combination fixture	Private	Faucet	2.25	2.25	3.0
Dishwashing machine	Private	Automatic		1.4	1.4
Drinking fountain	Offices, etc.	$3/8''$ valve	0.25		0.25
Kitchen sink	Private	Faucet	1.0	1.0	1.4
Kitchen sink	Hotel, restaurant	Faucet	3.0	3.0	4.0
Laundry trays (1 to 3)	Private	Faucet	1.0	1.0	1.4
Lavatory	Private	Faucet	0.5	0.5	0.7
Lavatory	Public	Faucet	1.5	1.5	2.0
Service sink	Offices, etc.	Faucet	2.25	2.25	3.0
Shower head	Public	Mixing valve	3.0	3.0	4.0
Shower head	Private	Mixing valve	1.0	1.0	1.4
Urinal	Public	1″ flush valve	10.0		10.0
Urinal	Public	$3/4''$ flush valve	5.0		5.0
Urinal	Public	Flush tank	3.0		3.0
Washing machine (8 lbs.)	Private	Automatic	1.0	1.0	1.4
Washing machine (8 lbs.)	Public	Automatic	2.25	2.25	3.0
Washing machine (15 lbs.)	Public	Automatic	3.0	3.0	4.0
Water closet	Private	Flush valve	6.0		6.0
Water closet	Private	Flush tank	2.2		2.2
Water closet	Public	Flush valve	10.0		10.0
Water closet	Public	Flush valve	5.0		5.0
Water closet	Public or private	Flushometer tank	2.0		2.0

For **SI:** 1 inch = 25.4 mm.

[a] For fixtures not listed, loads should be assumed by comparing the fixture to one listed using water in similar quantities and at similar rates. The assigned loads for fixtures with both hot and cold water supplies are given for separate hot and cold water loads and for total load, the separate hot and cold water loads being three-fourths of the total load for the fixture in each case.

Source: Courtesy of International Code Council. Reprinted from International Plumbing Code 1997 with permission.

demand for each in wsfu. The **load value** for each fixture is based upon the maximum amount of water that the fixture would require during use.

The actual sizing process for domestic water lines is really quite simple. We need to make just one simple choice concerning the type of fixtures being serviced, then we're off to sizing the pipe. Before sizing any branch we need to decide if the fixture to be supplied by the system at that point is primarily *flush tank* or *flush valve*. Notice the column labeled "Type of Supply Control" in Table 1.4. As a general rule we treat all fixtures not designated *flush valve* as *flush tank* fixtures. This will become an important step in our sizing procedure because flush valve fixtures require larger pipe sizes due to their higher water demand. For simplicity, the abbreviations **fv** for flush valve fixtures and **ft** for flush tank fixtures are often used.

A number of factors will affect the pressure in the water supply lines. Every time the pipe turns or a branch is created using a cross or tee, the water pressure will drop a bit. This is mainly due to friction between the water and the pipe or fitting. Valves also create a nominal pressure drop, as do significant vertical rises in pipe. For simplicity in this text we will study systems that require few special sizing considerations. All of our pipe sizes will come from Appendix B, which is based upon a pressure drop of 4 psi per 100 feet of pipe. There are many such tables available based on various pressure losses per 100 feet of pipe, and all are used in the same manner.

Finally, all we need to do in order to prepare our piping supply system for sizing is to assign the appropriate wsfu value to each individual length of piping. This is done in the following manner:

COLD WATER SUPPLY

1. Locate all plumbing fixtures.

2. Select the water system you wish to size — hot or cold.

3. Determine if each fixture is for *public* or *private* use (see "Occupancy" column in Table 1.4). A public use fixture will be found in a location accessible to the general public. Private fixtures will be located in offices or other private quarters.

4. Find each fixture name in the far left column of Table 1.4. Write the corresponding wsfu load value for the system you are sizing next to each fixture on the drawing (see Figure 1.46).

5. Write the letters *fv* next to all flush valve fixtures. (In most cases only water closets and urinals will be flush valve if specified for a particular job.)

FIGURE 1.46
Sample cold water layout.

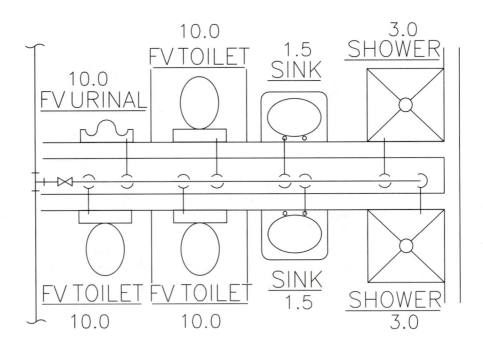

6. Beginning with the last fixture in each branch, write the number of wsfus serviced by each line. Be sure to add all new wsfu values each time you cross a line or branch (see Figure 1.47).

7. Finally, select the size pipe that corresponds to the wsfu number for each labeled pipe branch (shown in Figure 1.48).

Notice that the lines that run to the fixtures in the private bathroom have been sized using the *flush tank* column of the table in Appendix B. All of the other lines have been sized using the *flush*

FIGURE 1.47
Sample cold water layout with wsfu labels.

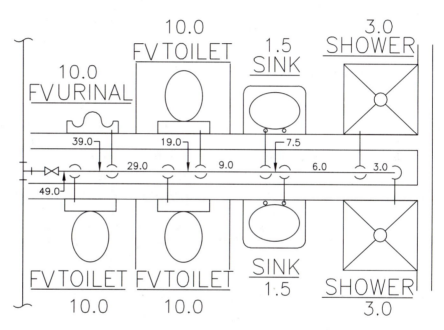

FIGURE 1.48
Sample layout with line sizes.

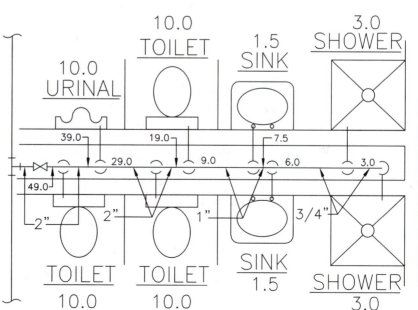

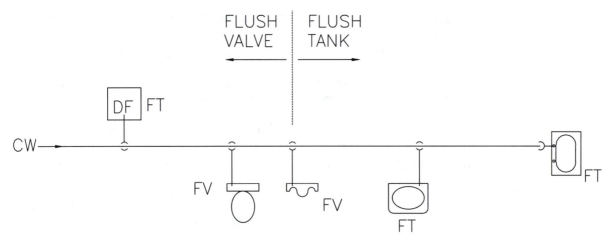

FIGURE 1.49
Cold water layout with flush tank and flush valve fixtures.

valve column because there are two flush valve water closets located downstream. Figure 1.49 shows a simple method for determining if a line should be sized as a flush valve or flush tank supply line. The solid lines represent all supply lines that lead directly to or service flush valve fixtures. The dashed lines show pipes that service all nonflush valve fixtures.

To size a *hot water system* we would used these same steps with the exception that no consideration needs to be taken for flush tank versus flush valve data. We simply size all pipes using the *flush tank* column.

Now let's look at some sample problems that make use of the information we have just examined.

Sample Problem   2.1

Figure 1.50 shows a partial plumbing layout for a building. The main supply line, shown at the top right-hand side, is required to deliver 60 gpm to the system. Determine the sizes for all of the supply piping shown. Below is a list of the fixtures used:

P-1:	Flush valve wall-mounted water closet (public)
P-1a:	Flush valve wall-mounted handicapped accessible water closet (public)
P-2:	1-in. flush valve wall-mounted urinal (public)
P-3:	Lavatory sink (public)
P-4:	Dual basin kitchen service sink (restaurant style)
EWC:	Electric water cooler

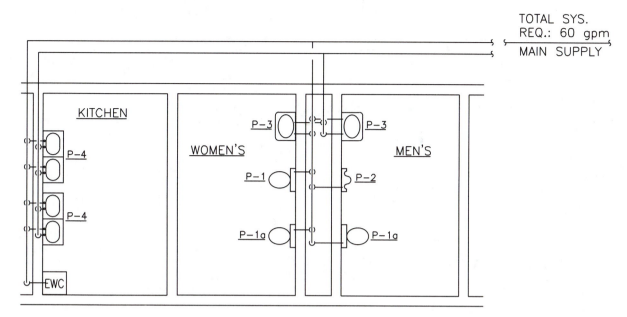

FIGURE 1.50
Sample plumbing layout.

Using Table 1.4 we assign the wsfu values to each fixture as follows:

P-1:   cold — 10.0   hot — n/a

P-1a: cold — 10.0   hot — n/a

P-2:   cold — 10.0   hot — n/a

P-3:   cold — 1.5   hot — 1.5

P-4:   cold — 3.0   hot — 3.0 (Values are per basin. Each fixture has two basins.)

EWC: cold — 0.25   hot — n/a

Notice that each fixture listed has the same wsfu values for both cold and hot water except for the bathroom groups. This is because a bathroom group is a combination fixture containing a water closet and a lavatory sink. Now, we write the wsfu value next to each fixture on the drawing as shown in Figure 1.51. Starting at the end of each branch of pipe, we now can assign the wsfu value for each segment of pipe by adding the wsfu values from each subsequent pipe branch in the manner explained earlier in this section. Because some of the wsfu values contain fractions, we will round up to the next whole number (shown in parentheses in Figure 1.51) to size each pipe.

Once all of the pipes have been assigned a wsfu value, we can use the table in Appendix B to find the required pipe size for each pipe. All cold water piping located between the water closets and the main supply

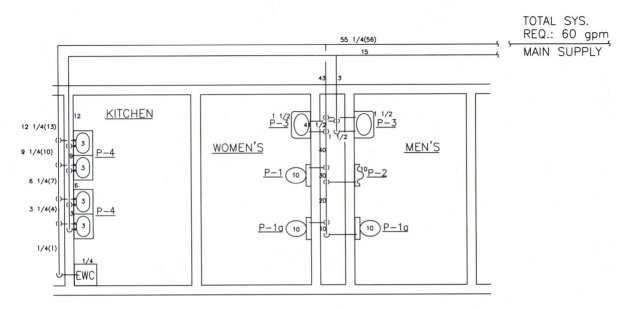

FIGURE 1.51
Sample layout with wsfu labels.

must be sized for flush valve fixtures because these lines all deliver water downstream to flush valve water closets and a urinal. Only the lines leading directly to the lavatory sinks will be sized as flush tank lines because they do not deliver water to any flush valve fixtures. All cold water piping located beyond the rest room branch may be sized using the *flush tank* column of Appendix B. Hot water lines are always sized using the *flush tank* column.

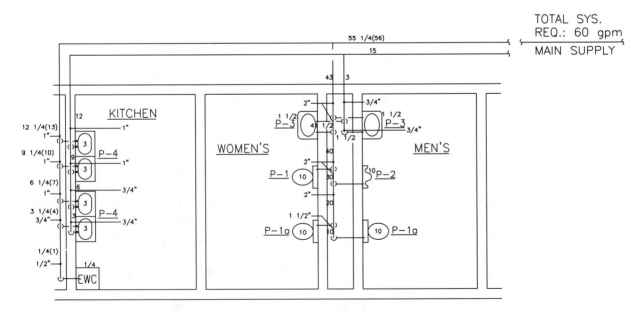

FIGURE 1.52
Sample layout with pipe sizes.

The resulting sizes are shown in Figure 1.52.

To determine the size of the supply main, we simply find the equivalent wsfu value for the total system demand of 60 gpm using Appendix A. Here we find that 61.0 gpm is equivalent to 180 wsfu. Because this system contains a number of flush valve fixtures, we must size the main as such. Referring to Appendix B we find that a flush valve system with a demand of 180 wsfu requires **2½-inch** diameter pipe.

Sample Problem **2.2**

Try to solve the following problem on your own. Then examine the solution that follows.

A 2-story hotel has 120 rooms. Forty of the rooms are on the first floor and the remaining 80 rooms are on the second floor. Each room typically contains 3 private fixtures: a shower, a flush tank water closet, and a lavatory sink. Each room is serviced by a single hot and cold water line that branches from a main running above the corridor ceiling on each floor. Determine the following:

a. typical pipe size for hot and cold water branches serving each room
b. largest size of hot and cold water mains for the first floor
c. largest size of hot and cold water mains for the second floor
d. total system demand in *gpm*
e. supply main size based on total system demand

Solution:

The wsfu ratings for each fixture mentioned are:

shower — 1.0 (cold and hot)

lavatory sink — 0.5 (cold and hot)

water closet — 2.2 (cold only)

a. Each room has a total demand of 3.7 wsfu (cold) and 1.5 wsfu (hot). Because there are no flush valve fixtures, all sizes will be based on the demand for flush tank fixtures. Referring to Appendix B, we find that a **¾-inch cold water line** and a **½-inch hot water line** will be sufficient to service each room.

b. The first floor contains 40 rooms. Therefore, the total demands for domestic water will be:

cold water — 40(3.7 wsfu) = 148 wsfu

hot water — 40(1.5 wsfu) = 60 wsfu

Referring again to Appendix B, we find the appropriate flush tank rated pipe sizes to be **2 inches for the cold water line** and **1½ inches for the hot water line**. Of course, the supply main will reduce in size as it runs down the corridor. These sizes represent the largest pipe needed (which would be the pipe size at the beginning of the service to this floor).

c. Because the second floor contains 80 rooms, which is twice as many as there are on the first floor, we can simply double the wsfu values that we found in part b:

cold water — 2(148 wsfu) = 296 wsfu

hot water — 2(60 wsfu) = 120 wsfu

From Appendix B we find that a **2½-inch cold water line** and a **2-inch hot water line** are required here.

d. To find the total system demand in gpm we must first compute the total system demand in wsfu. Because the building contains 120 rooms, we need only determine the total load for each room, then multiply the result by 120. Because the supply main delivers water to the building for use in both hot and cold water systems, it must be sized sufficiently for this purpose. Referring to Table 1.4 we use the far right column "Total" for this purpose.

shower — 1.4 (total)

lavatory sink — 0.7 (total)

water closet — 2.2 (total)

Therefore, the total water demand for one room is 4.3 wsfu. This makes the total demand for the entire building:

total demand = 120(4.3 wsfu) = 516 wsfu

To find the system demand in gpm we use Appendix A. Notice that there are no values between 500 wsfu and 750 wsfu. To find a value in between, we interpolate in the following manner:

$$
\begin{array}{r}
500 \text{ wsfu} = 124.0 \text{ gpm} \\
\underline{16 \text{ wsfu} = 18.0 \text{ gpm}} \\
516 \text{ wsfu} = \mathbf{142.0 \text{ gpm}}
\end{array}
$$

When using this method of interpolation be sure to use the largest single increment available. For example, to find the equivalent gpm for 223 wsfu, use 200 wsfu, 20 wsfu, and 3 wsfu. Look at the example below:

CORRECT		INCORRECT	
200 wsfu =	65.0 gpm	100 wsfu =	43.5 gpm
20 wsfu =	19.6 gpm	100 wsfu =	43.5 gpm
3 wsfu =	6.5 gpm	13 wsfu =	16.5 gpm
223 wsfu =	91.1 gpm	213 wsfu =	103.5 gpm

To use interpolation to find a missing wsfu value based on a known gpm value, refer to Appendix G.

---

e. Finally, to find the size of the supply main, we use Appendix B and the total demand of 516 wsfu from part d to find that a **3-inch pipe** is required.

Sample Problem   2.3

Solve the following problem on your own. Then, check your answer with the one found at the end of Part I.

A certain branch of pipe serves five fixtures in the following order (moving downstream):

1. a drinking fountain
2. a public flush valve water closet
3. a public flush valve urinal
4. a public lavatory sink
5. a service sink

Determine:

a. the appropriate size cold and hot water lines serving each fixture
b. the size of each segment of the pipe branch
c. the total demand in *gpm* for hot and cold water for this branch

HOT WATER RECIRCULATION SYSTEMS

Certain buildings have a large quantity of fixtures that utilize hot water. Some buildings contain fixtures that utilize hot water and are located a long distance from a hot water heater. Still other systems require the water in a hot water system to remain within a critical temperature range. Each of these systems would require a **hot water recirculation system**. A recirculation system is designed to allow water to flow back through the hot water heater occasionally so that it can remain at a desired temperature. Recirculation systems may operate in one of the following manners:

Timed recirculation — This type of system recirculates the water using an electronic timer and is activated at regular intervals.

Thermostatic — When the water at a specific location drops below a certain temperature, an electronic control activates the recirculation system. The water continues to recirculate until the desired temperature is reached.

Continuous — In systems where temperature maintenance is very critical, the water is constantly recirculated.

Figure 1.53 shows an example of a typical hot water recirculation system. If we follow the hot water line from the HWHTR, we find that it eventually comes to a pipe branch. On that branch we find a **bal-**

FIGURE 1.53
HWC line schematics.

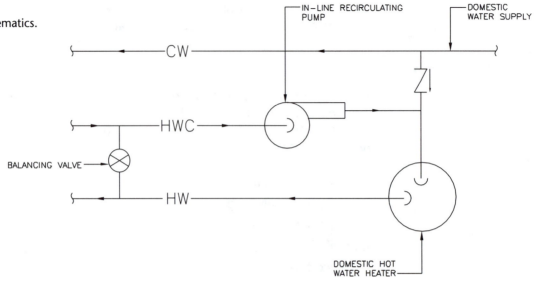

HOT WATER RECIRCULATION W/BALANCING VALVE

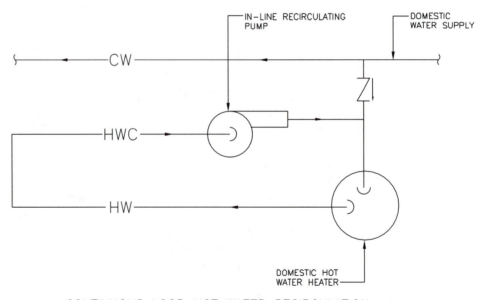

CONTINUOUS LOOP HOT WATER RECIRCULATION

ancing valve. This valve is designed to open when the recirculating pump is activated. The *balancing valve* will allow water to flow only from the hot water line to the hot water recirculating (HWC) line. In long pipe runs, several recirculation branches with balancing valves may be used so that the water in each segment or zone can begin recirculating immediately upon activation of the recirculating (recirc) pump. In shorter runs of pipe (usually 100 feet or less), we can design the hot water line and recirc line as a single, continuous loop (also shown in Figure 1.53).

Be careful not to confuse *continuous recirculation* with a *continuous loop.* Continuous or constant recirculation means that the water in the recirc line is constantly flowing because the pump never shuts down. A continuous recirculation loop (illustrated in Figure 1.53) is simply a pipe loop that runs into the system and doubles back at some point to return to the hot water heater.

A detail of a typical domestic water supply system with a recirc line is shown in Figure 1.54. This particular detail shows an **automatic temperature control (ATC)** recirculation system. In an ATC system one or more **temperature sensors (TS)** are located along the HW line. Each is electonically tied in to an ATC switch for the recirc pump through a sensor relay. When one of the sensors reads a line temperature below the programmed range, a signal is sent through the relay and the ATC switch activates the pump until the TS reads the appropriate higher temperature. Then, a second signal is sent to the ATC, which opens the switch and turns the pump off.

For example, if the ATC on a particular 120°F recirc line were set to operate in the range of 118°F to 125°F, then the circuit would be closed and the pump would come on when the line temperature read below 118°F. Likewise, the pump would remain on until the signal from the TS indicated that the temperature in the line had reached 125°F.

Sizing a hot water recirculation line is not difficult at all. In fact, it's actually easier than sizing a hot water main. All we need to know is the volumetric flow rating of the recirc pump. Then we can find the equivalent wsfu value in Appendix A under the column for predominantly flush tank fixtures. Finally, we use the table in Appendix C to find the pipe size. To use this table we must know the pump flow rate and the allowable amount of pressure drop per 100 feet of pipe in *psi*. For example, to find out the size of a recirc line needed for an 8 gpm recirc pump if the allowable pressure loss in the HWC line were 10 psi per 100 feet, we would consult Appendix C as follows:

1. Find the pressure loss value in psi along the bottom of the chart.

2. Move up the dashed line that represents your allowable pressure loss until you reach the pump flow rate line (marked on both left and right sides of the chart).

3. From the point you located in step 2, move upward until you reach the first **bold** line that runs upward and to the right. **Read the pipe diameter on the top of this line.**

Following the procedure outlined above, we can find the size of the recirc line for our example.

1. The allowable pressure drop is 10 psi/100 ft.

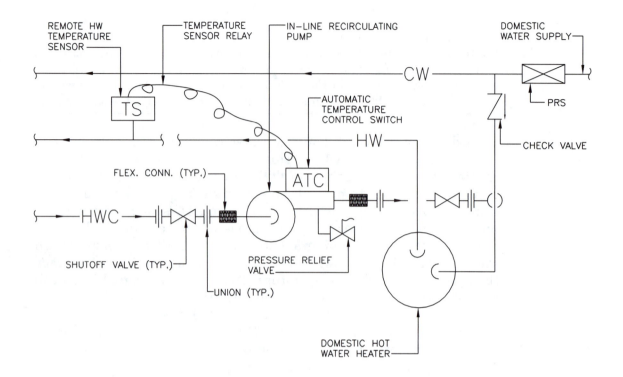

TYPICAL ATC HOT WATER RECIRCULATION DETAIL

FIGURE 1.54
ATC HWC system schematic.

2. Move up the dashed 10 psi line until you reach the 8 gpm horizontal line.

3. You should now be located just below the bold line labeled "¾ inch."

Therefore, you would need a **¾-inch** diameter HWC line for this system.

Most recirculation lines turn out to be relatively small in diameter compared to the actual hot water line sizes because they are designed to carry only enough water to reheat the existing water in the line. This amounts to only a small fraction of the amount of water needed to supply the fixtures utilizing hot water.

Hot water recirculation systems can also be based upon a specific fraction or percentage of the HW supply being provided at all points along the supply line. In these instances the HWC line must be sized in segments. Let's use the diagram shown in Figure 1.55 for our next example. In this diagram we are showing only the hot water mains and the hot water recirc line throughout this building. The total wsfu rating for each HW branch is noted at the pipe breaks, and all of the HW pipe sizes have been indicated.

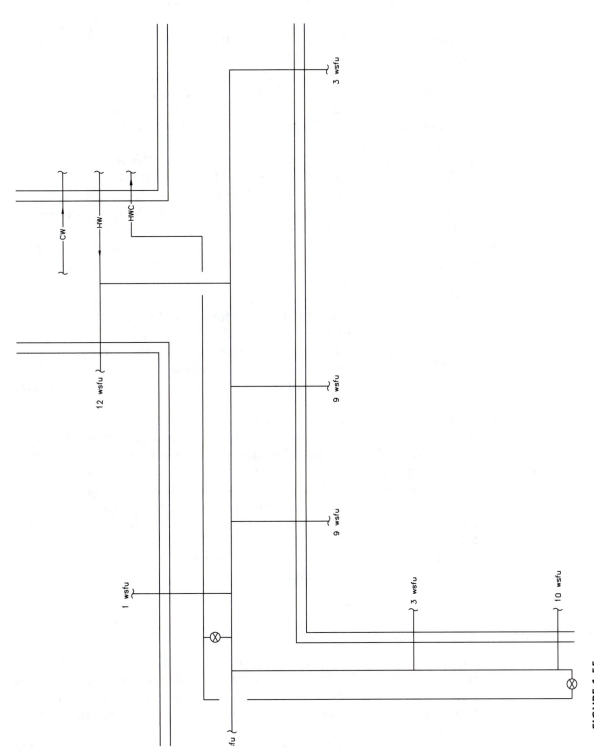

FIGURE 1.55
Example illustration.

Let's assume that we need to recirculate the hot water in this system at a rate of 30% of the system demand and the maximum allowable pressure loss is 10 psi/100 feet. First, we need to place our recirculation branches and tie them into the HW main. We want to do this at the end of long runs or after several groups of takeoffs so that each branch is serving zones or regions that have similar demands. The total HW system demand is 53 wsfu. Using Appendix A we find that this equates to 35.6 gpm. Because 30% of 35.6 gpm is 10.68 gpm, we will use Appendix C to find the size pipe needed to deliver 11 gpm (rounded up from 10.68 gpm) with a pressure loss of 10 psi/100 feet of pipe. This yields an initial pipe size of **1 inch** for the HWC line.

Moving farther down the line we find that HWC branch tie-ins have been placed along the 1½-inch main just beyond the 12 wsfu and 3 wsfu takeoffs. This means that 15 wsfu are no longer being served by the next run of the HWC. This leaves 38 wsfu downstream of the branch. Using Appendix A we find that this is equivalent to 31.4 gpm, and 30% of this value yields 10 gpm when rounded up. Appendix C tells us that 10 gpm at 10 psi drop/100 feet requires a **1-inch** pipe as well.

The final branch is located at the far left of the horizontal run and leaves only 19 wsfu downstream. Using the same procedure just described, we find that 19 wsfu equates to 19.2 gpm, which yields a 6 gpm HWC line demand. Appendix C reveals that the size for this pipe needs to be **3/4 -inch**. The final result with all sizes provided is shown in Figure 1.56.

Again, notice that we divided the HW system into roughly equal zones (15 wsfu, 19 wsfu, and 19 wsfu). This is a good practice whenever possible. Another consideration to remember is that overall pipe length, pipe rises and drops, and valves and fittings all create pressure drops. Section 9 of the International Plumbing Code describes in detail how to account for these conditions. For the purpose of simplicity, however, these items have not been included in the scope of this text.

Now let's look at some sample problems to see how these principles apply to a domestic hot water system.

Sample Problem   2.4

A continuous loop hot water recirculation line in a restaurant serves a row of 10 kitchen service sinks, 5 dishwashers, and a 5 gpm secondary hot water heater at 10% of demand. Assuming a negligible pressure loss due to valves, fittings, and overall pipe length, size the HWC line using a pressure loss of 10 psi/100 ft.

First, we'll determine the total demand in *wsfu* using Table 1.4 (excluding the HWHTR):

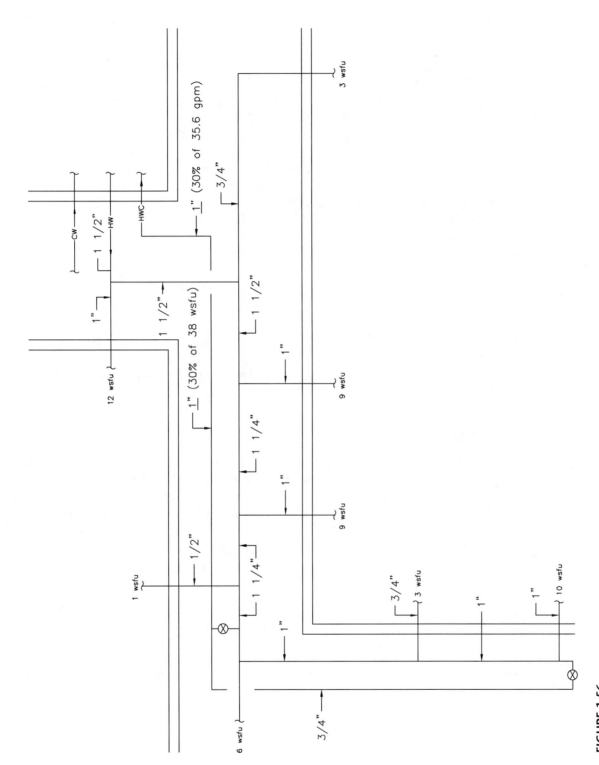

FIGURE 1.56
Example illustration with pipe sizes.

10 kitchen service sinks:	10(3.0 wsfu) =	30.0 wsfu
5 dishwashing machines:	5(1.4 wsfu) =	7.0 wsfu
	Total:	37.0 wsfu

Next, we need to convert the system wsfu rating into *gpm*. We also need to remember to add the gpm rating for the HWHTR at this time. Using Appendix A we find that: 37.0 wsfu = 35.0 wsfu + 2 wsfu = 24.9 gpm + 5.0 gpm = 34.9 gpm. Adding the 5 gpm for the HWHTR, we arrive at 39.9 gpm for total HW demand.

Because the HWC demand is 10% of the HW system demand, we'll be using 3.99 or 4 gpm as our HWC system demand. From Appendix C we find that this demand at a pressure loss of 10 psi/100 feet requires a **5/8-inch HWC pipe**. Because a 3/4-inch diameter pipe is a more common size, we might suggest this size instead.

Sample Problem 2.5

Try to solve the following problem on your own. Then examine the solution that follows. Figure 1.57 shows a domestic hot water supply system and a hot water recirculation main. Use three branch tie-ins to connect the HWC line to the HW line. Then, size the HWC lines based on 20 psi loss/100 feet and 20% demand recirculation.

Solution:

To begin this problem we can compute the total system HW demand in *wsfu* so that we can determine the best locations for our HWC branches. Remember, we want to divide the system up as evenly as possible. Adding all of the wsfu values shown in Figure 1.57, we find that the total HW demand is 64 wsfu. Because the problem asks us to divide the system into three branches, we want to keep each branch as close to 21.3 wsfu

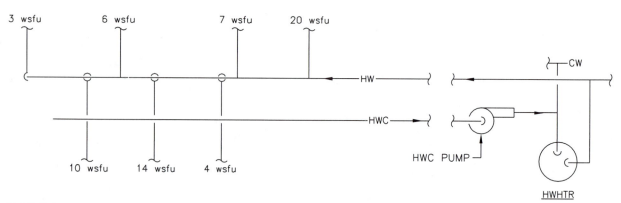

FIGURE 1.57
Sample problem illustrations.

(64 wsfu/3 branches) as possible. Using this value for each branch, we find that the first branch should be placed just after the 20 wsfu HW branch. The next three HW branches total 25 wsfu, which is also very close to 21.3; therefore, we'll place the next HWC branch after the 14 wsfu HW branch. This leaves 19 wsfu for the final branch, which we'll tie in near the end of the HW line (see Figure 1.58).

With the HWC tie-ins now in place we can proceed to size the branches. Because the total system rating is 64 wsfu, we will use Appendix A and the procedure previously described to determine the equivalent gpm demand. To find this value we need to add 32.0 gpm (60 wsfu) and 8.0 gpm (4 wsfu) to get 40 gpm, 20% of which is 8 gpm. Using Appendix C at 20 psi loss/100 feet, we find that a **5/8-inch pipe** will be sufficient for this application. The next branch is at 44 wsfu, which equates to 34.3 gpm, and 20% of this value is 7 gpm (6.86 rounded up). Again, a **5/8-inch pipe** will be sufficient for this application. Finally, the remaining segment is rated at 19 wsfu, which is equivalent to 19.2 gpm. When we compute 20% of this value we find the final HWC demand is 4 gpm (rounded up from 3.84). Appendix C tells us that a **1/2-inch pipe** is needed here.

Sample Problem   2.6

Solve the following problem on your own. Then, check your answer with the one found at the end of Part I.

Determine the appropriate gpm rating for the recirc pump in Sample Problem 2.5 if the pressure loss were reduced to 10 psi/100 feet (assume the same size HWC main).

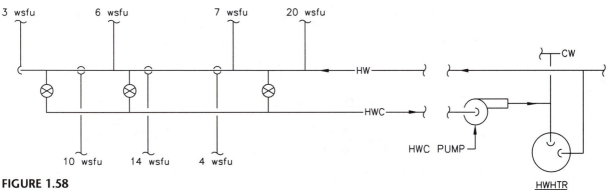

FIGURE 1.58
Sample problem illustrations with HWC branches added.

DOMESTIC WATER PLUMBING PLANS

We call the standard single-line layouts of piping that are superimposed on a floor plan or part plan of a building a **plumbing plan**. As you have probably noticed by this time, plumbing plans are schematic in nature. We don't show the true thickness for each pipe, we don't draw items such as valves or fittings in any great detail, and we exaggerate pipe rise and drop circle sizes for clarity. Domestic water plumbing drawings in general rely heavily on the use of symbols. Although many common symbols are used throughout the industry, each individual company or consultant has the right to use any set of symbols he or she chooses. For this reason all complete sets of plumbing drawings for any project should include a **symbols legend**. A legend lists all of the symbols and abbreviations for terms as they appear typically on all of the drawings. An example of a plumbing symbols legend is shown in Figure 1.59.

Another important aspect of domestic plumbing plans is the **order of assembly**. When we show items on a plumbing plan, we locate them in the order in which they are to be installed. We also try to locate these items as close as possible to their intended location; however, due to the size of the symbols this is not always practical.

FIGURE 1.59
Sample plumbing legend.

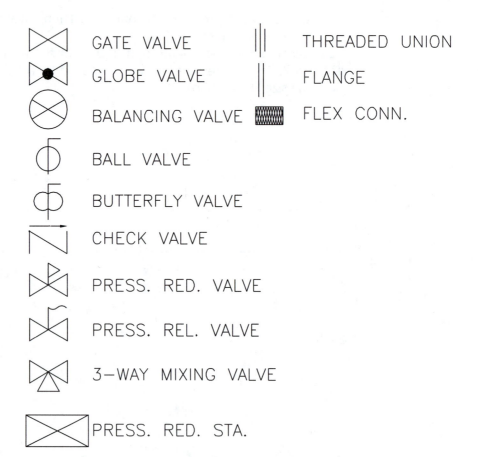

The purpose for the plumbing plan is to show pipe routing and relative locations for plumbing fixtures. For exact locations of the plumbing fixtures, we would consult a set of dimensioned architectural drawings. These drawings would show us the exact placement of the fixtures relative to the closest walls or partitions. The plumbing plan also uses **labels** for each of the fixtures in the building. Figure 1.60, for example, shows a pair of rest rooms that share a common wall. The chart that accompanies the drawing is called a **plumbing fixture schedule** and is used to briefly describe each of the fixtures labeled in the plumbing plan. Although a schedule may contain more information than is shown in this diagram, all fixture plumbing schedules contain essentially the same information:

1. A description of each fixture is provided.

2. The size of the cold water and/or hot water connections are provided.

3. Additional information about the fixture may also be provided.

The description is obvious for each item. This column simply lists the name of each fixture. The water line connection columns (CW and HW) are taken from the **manufacturer's specifications** and are not determined by the supply sizing method described previously in this text. The "Remarks" column offers the designer/engineer the opportunity to provide additional comments about each fixture. As we shall see in the section "Sanitary Waste and Vent Systems," the plumbing schedule may be expanded to include drain/waste connections as well.

For the sake of efficiency, each individual fixture is not usually given a unique label. Rather, all common fixtures are given the same label for consistency. For example, Figure 1.60 contains a total of eight fixtures; however, the schedule has only four fixture descriptions. Looking more carefully at Figure 1.60, we see that it actually contains one urinal (P-2), two lavatory sinks (P-3), two handicapped-accessible water closets (P-1a), and three standard water closets (P-1). By the way, all plumbing fixture labels are arbitrarily assigned (i.e., a certain company may use P-3 for a lavatory sink whereas another company uses P-5 for the same fixture).

So far, we have seen how to represent piping layouts on a floor plan; however, this is not the only way to represent the routing of piping in a plumbing system. In the next section, we investigate another type of diagram that is commonly used to identify pipe sizes and clarify pipe routing.

TOPICAL QUESTIONS

Answer the following questions to the best of your ability based on the material covered in this portion of the text. Then check your answers with those found at the end of Part I.

FIGURE 1.60
Plumbing part floor plan.

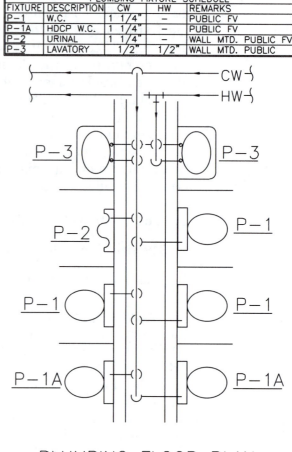

PLUMBING FIXTURE SCHEDULE				
FIXTURE	DESCRIPTION	CW	HW	REMARKS
P–1	W.C.	1 1/4"	–	PUBLIC FV
P–1A	HDCP W.C.	1 1/4"	–	PUBLIC FV
P–2	URINAL	1 1/4"	–	WALL MTD. PUBLIC FV
P–3	LAVATORY	1/2"	1/2"	WALL MTD. PUBLIC

PLUMBING FLOOR PLAN

1. Briefly describe a domestic water plumbing plan.

2. Where would you find a list of plumbing symbols used in a particular set of drawings?

3. What is a plumbing fixture label?

DOMESTIC WATER RISER DIAGRAMS

A **riser diagram** can be thought of as a road map for the plumbing system. Figure 1.61 shows an example of a **standard domestic water plumbing riser diagram**. This diagram is based on the plumbing floor plan found in Figure 1.60. Figure 1.62 shows the same layout in an **isometric riser diagram**.

The method for generating a standard domestic water plumbing riser diagram is not difficult if we follow a few simple rules:

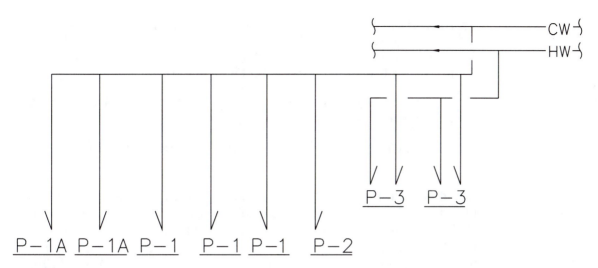

FIGURE 1.61
Standard domestic water riser.

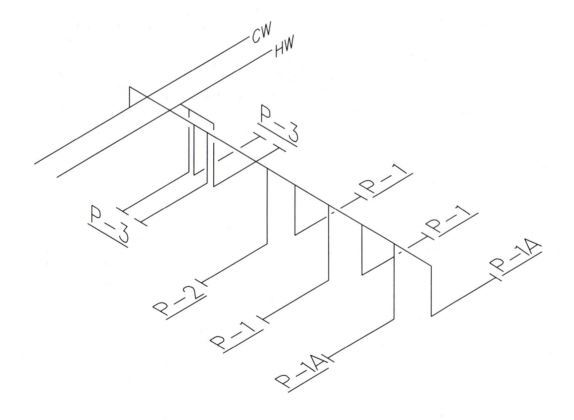

ISOMETRIC PLUMBING RISER

FIGURE 1.62
Isometric riser.

1. All vertical lines represent takeoffs, not pipe rises or drops.

2. Pipe branches and fixtures always turn in the direction of the branch or takeoff in the direction of water flow.

3. All horizontal runs of pipe are shown stacked regardless of actual pipe elevation.

4. Fixtures are indicated by labels only and are shown at relative elevations.

To generate a domestic water riser diagram from a domestic water plumbing plan, we first need to establish the direction of water flow. Then, we treat the pipe like a roadway. Driving through the pipe in the direction of water flow, we determine the direction of each takeoff by the direction we need to turn into each branch. Figure 1.63 highlights the path of one of the cold water branches in both the plan view and the riser diagram. The same path has been highlighted in the isometric riser shown in Figure 1.64.

Remember, all *vertical lines* on a riser diagram represent *takeoffs*, and all *horizontal turns* represent the *direction* of the pipe run. Figures 1.65 and 1.66 continue to trace the path of the cold water line up to fixture P-2 (urinal). Notice that the little tick mark at the end of each line (looks like a check mark) is turned in the direction in which the fixture is facing. Again, be sure to identify the direction of the takeoff by the direction you would need to turn to follow that takeoff while traveling through the pipe *in the direction of water flow*.

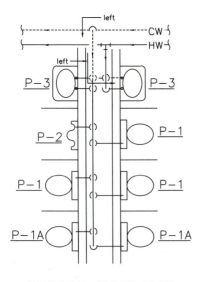

FIGURE 1.63
Riser with turns and takeoffs.

FIGURE 1.64
Isometric riser.

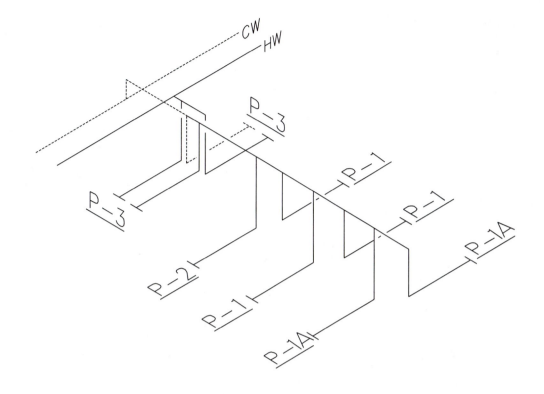

ISOMETRIC PLUMBING RISER

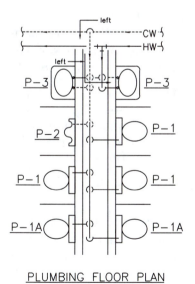

PLUMBING FLOOR PLAN

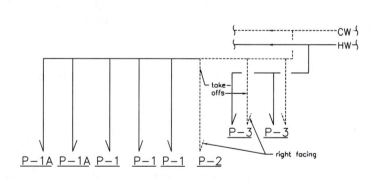

STANDARD PLUMBING RISER

FIGURE 1.65
Riser continuation.

FIGURE 1.66
Isometric riser
continuation.

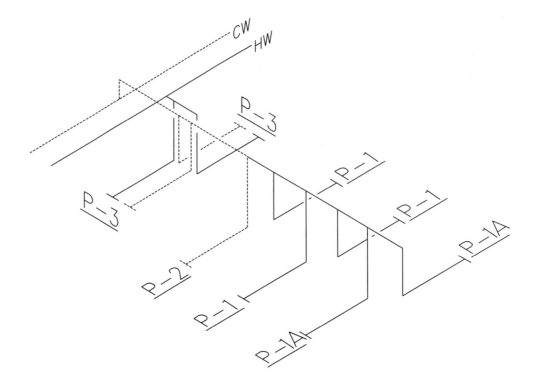

ISOMETRIC PLUMBING RISER

Figures 1.67 and 1.68 trace the completion of the cold water line. The hot water line (not highlighted) is run in exactly the same manner. Notice that where hot and cold water lines cross on the riser diagram, one of the lines is broken around the other. This is to indicate that the lines do not cross at that point.

Pipe sizing is often done using riser diagrams instead of plumbing plans because there is more space on the drawing for design notes. Also, riser diagrams are often more clear concerning vertical connections and order of assembly.

Two-story domestic water risers are generated in almost the same manner as one-story diagrams. Figure 1.69 shows the first- and second-floor plumbing plans for a small building and the isometric riser for the same building. Figure 1.70 illustrates a portion of the cold water line in a riser diagram with the same path highlighted in the plan and isometric views. Notice that the line makes a left turn (sometimes called "looking" left) immediately after it feeds the first hose bibb (H.B.) on the plumbing plan; however, the same line on the standard riser appears as a single straight line.

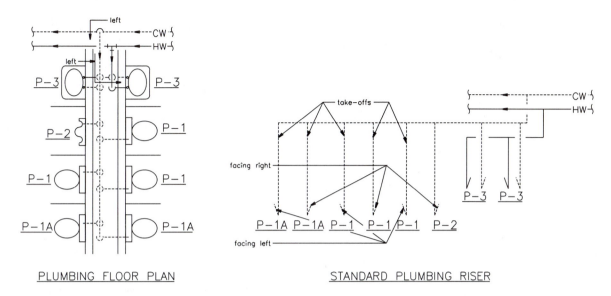

PLUMBING FLOOR PLAN   STANDARD PLUMBING RISER

FIGURE 1.67
Diagram with complete CW system highlighted.

FIGURE 1.68
Isometric riser.

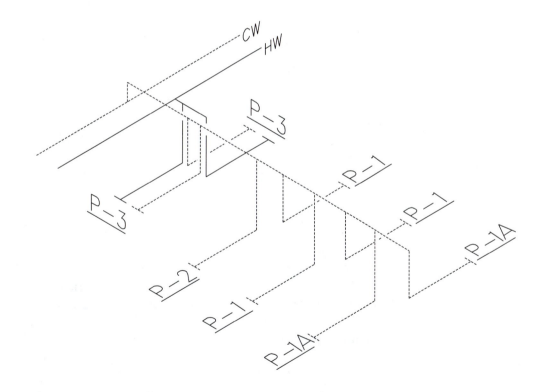

ISOMETRIC PLUMBING RISER

FIGURE 1.69
Two-story plumbing
plan.

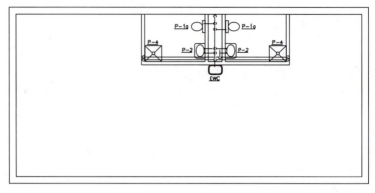

SECOND-FLOOR PLUMBING PLAN

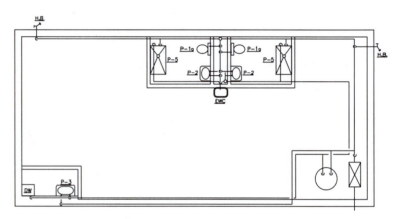

FIRST-FLOOR PLUMBING PLAN

FIGURE 1.69
Two-story plumbing
plan.

Regardless of the number of turns that a single pipe makes on a floor plan or elevation drawing, it will always appear as a single straight line on a riser diagram.

Continuing along the same cold water line, we can follow the generated riser diagram (Figure 1.71) and the remainder of the same line highlighted on the isometric riser. Figure 1.72 follows the lower portion of the first-floor cold water line and the part of the same line that extends upward to serve the second floor. To indicate that more than one floor is being serviced by this system, we use a horizontal line on the riser diagram to represent the relative location of each floor. The vertical takeoff that runs to the second floor is represented by a single vertical line on the riser diagram that crosses the second floor line. Notice that the portion of the riser diagram that is located above the second floor line is generated in the same manner as the riser for a single floor.

Finally, we can add the hot water line as discussed previously to complete the riser diagram. The result is shown in Figure 1.73.

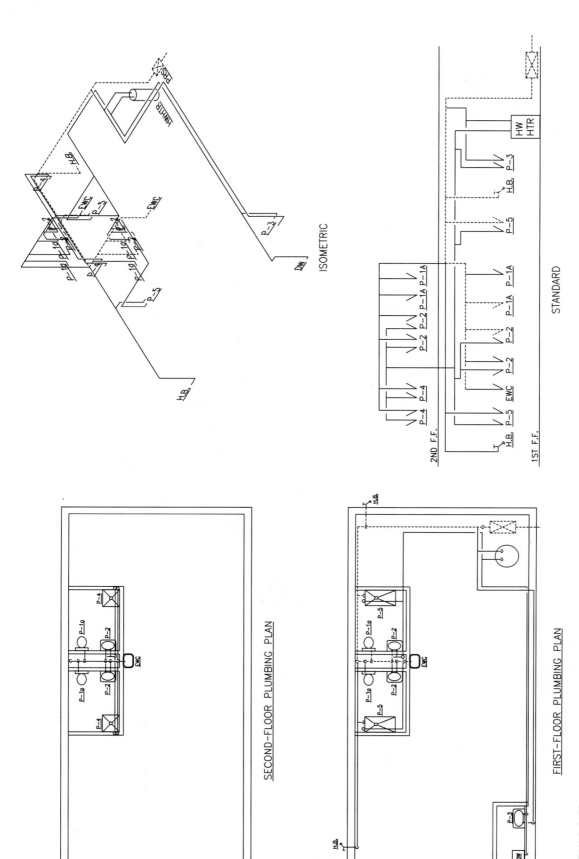

FIGURE 1.70
Plumbing plan with risers.

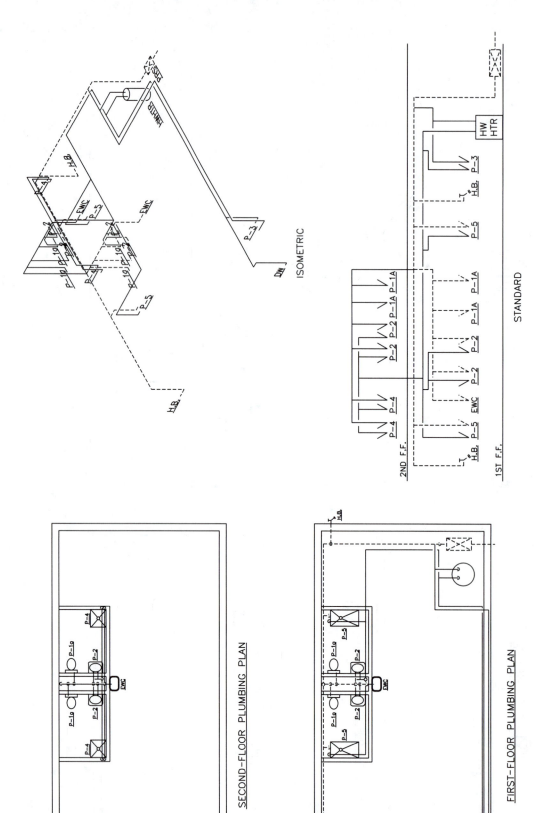

FIGURE 1.71
Plumbing plan with risers.

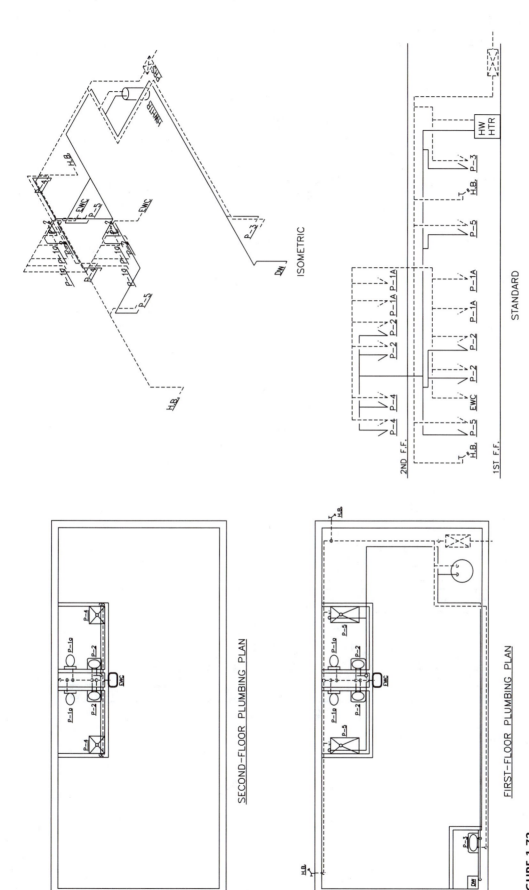

FIGURE 1.72
Plumbing plan with risers.

ISOMETRIC

STANDARD

SECOND-FLOOR PLUMBING PLAN

FIRST-FLOOR PLUMBING PLAN

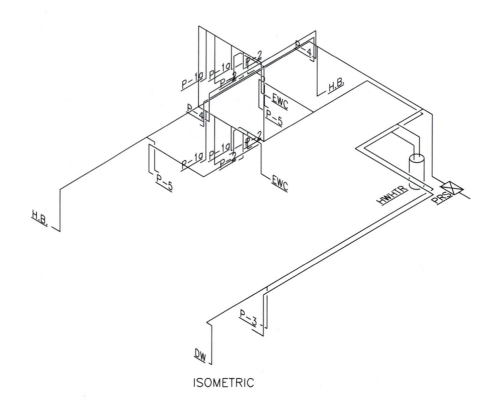

ISOMETRIC

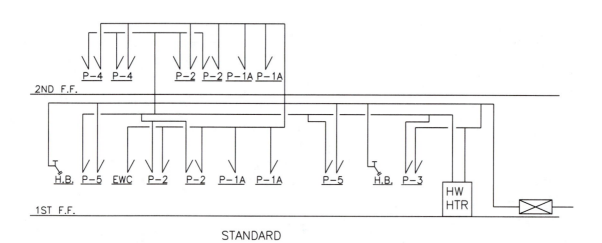

STANDARD

FIGURE 1.73
Completed risers.

TOPICAL QUESTIONS

Answer the following questions to the best of your ability based on the material covered in this portion of the text. Then check your answers with those found at the end of Part I.

1. What is the primary purpose for a domestic water plumbing riser diagram?

2. Explain the difference between a standard riser diagram and an isometric riser diagram.

3. Why might a designer choose to use a standard riser diagram instead of a plumbing plan to size pipes?

MISCELLANEOUS CONSIDERATIONS

A variety of other concerns need to be taken into account when designing a domestic water supply plumbing system. We will briefly address a number of these in this section.

Pipe Insulation

The purpose of pipe **insulation** is to prevent or retard the transfer of heat through the pipe wall. Simply put, insulation helps cold fluids in the pipe stay cold and keeps hot fluids hot. Insulation may also be used to prevent condensation from forming on the outside of a pipe when there is a significant amount of moisture in the air surrounding the pipe. Figure 1.74 illustrates an insulated length of pipe.

Hangers, Anchors, Riser Clamps, and Pipe Guides

There are a number of conventional methods used to hang or hold piping in place inside a building. One common method is the use of a **hanger**. This device, as its name implies, is used to hang pipe from an overhead structure, such as a wood truss, steel beam, or ceiling surface. Figure 1.75 shows a common type of hanger used in the industry.

FIGURE 1.74
Insulated pipe.

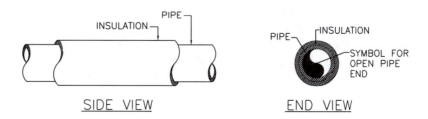

FIGURE 1.75
Pipe hanger.

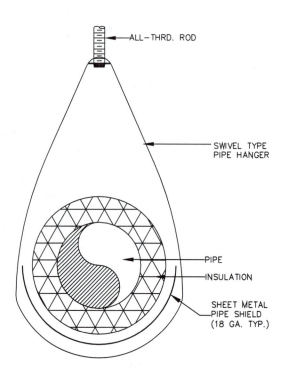

ALL-THRD. ROD

SWIVEL TYPE
PIPE HANGER

PIPE

INSULATION

SHEET METAL
PIPE SHIELD
(18 GA. TYP.)

TYPICAL PIPE HANGER DETAIL

SCALE: NONE

When a pipe is not insulated, the hanger selected will have the same diameter as the outer diameter of the pipe it is used to support. However, when we use a hanger to support an insulated pipe, we must provide a **pipe shield** that has the same diameter as the insulation on the outside of the pipe (see Figure 1.76). The size of the hanger required for this application will be determined by the overall diameter of the pipe after it has been insulated.

Another kind of hanger is the **roller hanger**. This kind of hanger allows lateral movement of the pipe along its line of run. Roller hangers are commonly used for hot water lines where thermal expansion may cause the pipe to move as it experiences changes in temperature. The criteria for selecting a roller hanger are the same as those for selecting a standard pipe hanger.

In order to attach a hanger to the building structure, we need to use a clamp or flange (shown in Figure 1.77). A **beam clamp** can be used to attach a hanger to a steel beam or steel joist. A **ceiling flange**, on the other hand, may be used when the hanger assembly must be attached to a flat surface such as a ceiling or subfloor.

FIGURE 1.76
Pipe shield.

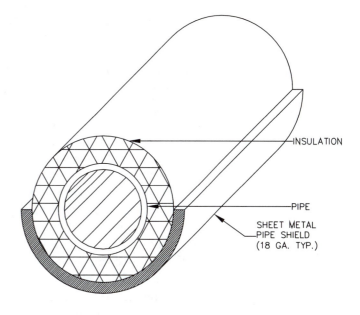

INSULATION

PIPE

SHEET METAL
PIPE SHIELD
(18 GA. TYP.)

TYPICAL PIPE SHIELD DETAIL
SCALE: NONE

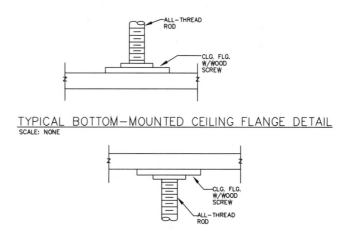

ALL-THREAD
ROD

CLG. FLG.
W/WOOD
SCREW

TYPICAL BOTTOM-MOUNTED CEILING FLANGE DETAIL
SCALE: NONE

CLG. FLG.
W/WOOD
SCREW

ALL-THREAD
ROD

TYPICAL TOP-MOUNTED CEILING FLANGE DETAIL
SCALE: NONE

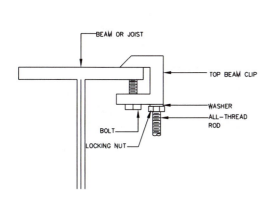

BEAM OR JOIST

TOP BEAM CLIP

WASHER

ALL-THREAD
ROD

BOLT

LOCKING NUT

TYPICAL TOP BEAM CLAMP DETAIL
SCALE: NONE

FIGURE 1.77
Beam clamp and ceiling flange.

If there is a risk of significant lateral movement of a pipe, which cannot be allowed because the pipe may become damaged or may damage other items, we need to use **pipe anchors** to hold it stationary. A pipe anchor, such as the one shown in Figure 1.78, is designed to prevent any movement of the pipe due to thrust forces (caused by the velocity of the fluid in the pipe) or expansion (caused by temperature increases inside the pipe).

Riser clamps are used to hold vertically running pipes in place against a wall or other stationary structure. The selection and sizing of riser clamps is the same as that for a pipe hanger. Shielding must be used on insulated vertical pipes where they are held in place by riser clamps. This kind of pipe support may strap directly to a wall (shown in Figure 1.79), or it may rest atop another surface (see the two-sided riser clamp shown in Figure 1.80).

When we simply need to maintain a pipe run along a certain path, we can make use of **pipe guides** as shown in Figure 1.81. Pipe guides are not designed to support the load of a pipe and its contents, nor are they designed to prevent the pipe from moving completely. Instead, pipe guides are simply used to align and maintain the alignment of pipes along a run.

Additional Methods of Pipe Mounting

In addition to the more conventional methods of pipe mounting listed previously, the designer and contractor can consider a few other options when deciding on methods for pipe installation.

One such method is the **trapeze**, shown in Figure 1.82. This installation method allows several pipes to be hung on the same apparatus. Using a trapeze can save a considerable amount of time, labor, and material because so many individual hangers are not needed.

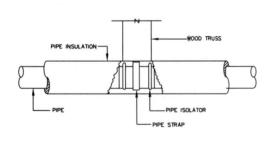

TYPICAL PIPE ANCHOR DETAIL
SCALE: NONE

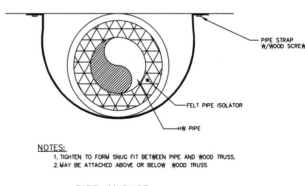

NOTES:
1. TIGHTEN TO FORM SNUG FIT BETWEEN PIPE AND WOOD TRUSS.
2. MAY BE ATTACHED ABOVE OR BELOW WOOD TRUSS.

PIPE ANCHOR
SCALE: NONE

FIGURE 1.78
Pipe anchors.

FIGURE 1.79
Strap type riser clamp.

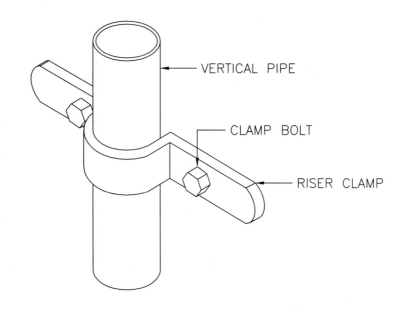

STRAP TYPE RISER CLAMP

FIGURE 1.80
Two-sided riser clamp.

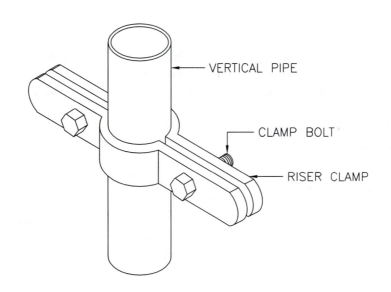

TWO—SIDED RISER CLAMP

FIGURE 1.81
Pipe guide.

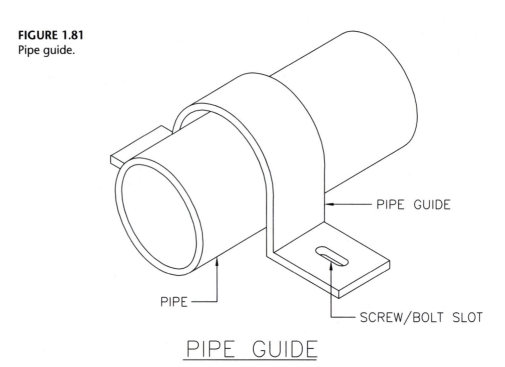

PIPE GUIDE

PIPE

SCREW/BOLT SLOT

PIPE GUIDE

However, a trapeze is not ideal in all situations. This configuration forces all of the pipes to have the same invert elevation, which may not always be desirable. The trapeze is also limited in strength by the materials available to be used. Also, many local codes do not allow the use of trapeze hangers for certain kinds of pipes or for pipes that are insulated.

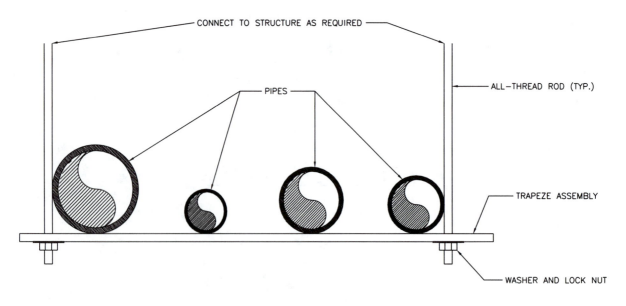

CONNECT TO STRUCTURE AS REQUIRED

PIPES

ALL–THREAD ROD (TYP.)

TRAPEZE ASSEMBLY

WASHER AND LOCK NUT

TRAPEZE HANGER

FIGURE 1.82
Trapeze.

The **slotted angle**, shown in Figure 1.83, is another method that can be used to support domestic water pipes. The slotted angle is nailed or screwed to two adjoining structural wood members. This creates a support upon which piping can be run.

In still another scenario a two-by-four is nailed across two wooden structural members. This kind of support, shown in Figure 1.84, is known as a **cross brace.**

Pipes also can be aligned vertically using a system called **stacking**. In the illustration shown in Figure 1.85 each pipe below the uppermost pipe uses the pipe immediately above it for support.

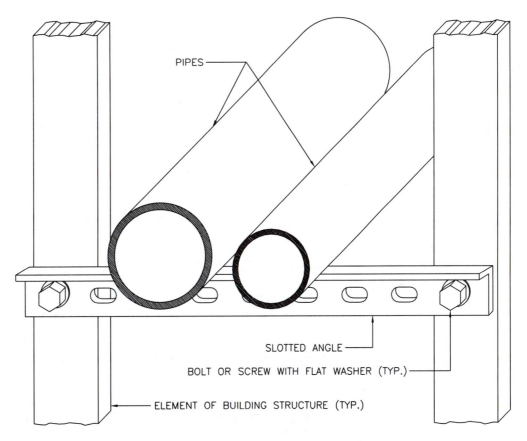

PIPES

SLOTTED ANGLE

BOLT OR SCREW WITH FLAT WASHER (TYP.)

ELEMENT OF BUILDING STRUCTURE (TYP.)

SLOTTED ANGLE HANGER

FIGURE 1.83
Slotted angle.

FIGURE 1.84
Cross brace.

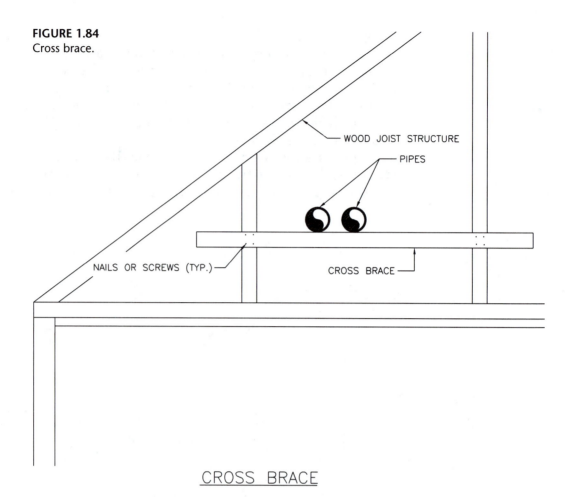

CROSS BRACE

TOPICAL QUESTIONS

Answer the following questions to the best of your ability based on the material covered in this portion of the text. Then check your answers with those found at the end of Part I.

1. Name two purposes that pipe insulation can serve.

2. When should a pipe shield be used to hang a pipe?

3. List an appropriate application for each of the following:
   a. roller hanger
   b. pipe guide
   c. trapeze hanger

FIGURE 1.85
Pipe stacking.

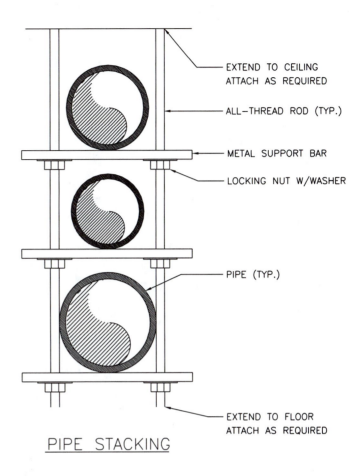

EXTEND TO CEILING
ATTACH AS REQUIRED

ALL—THREAD ROD (TYP.)

METAL SUPPORT BAR

LOCKING NUT W/WASHER

PIPE (TYP.)

EXTEND TO FLOOR
ATTACH AS REQUIRED

PIPE STACKING

SECTION 3

Sanitary Waste and Vent Systems

The counterpart to the domestic water plumbing supply system is the sanitary waste and vent system. The purpose of this system is to remove wastewater and other waste products from the plumbing fixtures in a building. However, unlike supply piping, the pipes in a sanitary waste system are sloped in the direction of waste flow making this a **gravometric** system (one that operates by using gravity). Vent piping is used to maintain a proper system pressure balance by allowing air to enter into and escape from the waste system. In this section we examine the application, layout, and sizing of this two-part system.

SANITARY WASTE SYSTEM DESIGN AND APPLICATIONS

Piping for the **sanitary waste system** is connected directly to one of the three following items:

1. a plumbing fixture drain

2. a floor drain

3. a clean out

Most of us are familiar with the **drains** on common plumbing fixtures, such as a sink drain, a water closet (toilet) drain, or a bathtub drain. This is the opening in a plumbing fixture that allows waste to escape into the sanitary waste system. Other than the drain valve on a fixture that remains closed to retain water (see the lavatory sink in Figure 1.86), a sanitary waste system inside a building does not generally use any valving.

FIGURE 1.86
Lavatory sink with drain.

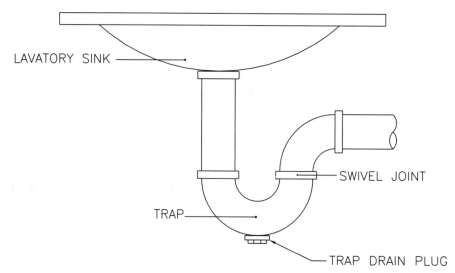

LAVATORY SINK

SWIVEL JOINT

TRAP

TRAP DRAIN PLUG

Floor drains (shown in Figure 1.87) are placed in locations where water is likely to accumulate at the floor level. Floor drains are commonly used in rest rooms, locker rooms, public showers, laundry rooms, and mechanical equipment rooms. The size of the floor drain needed for a particular application is based upon the potential rate at which water can accumulate in a given space. The branch connected to a floor drain will always be the same size as the drain itself.

A **clean out** is a capped opening that allows a plumber to have direct access to a sanitary pipe. Clean outs, such as the one shown in Figure 1.88, are always located upstream of the waste flow and may

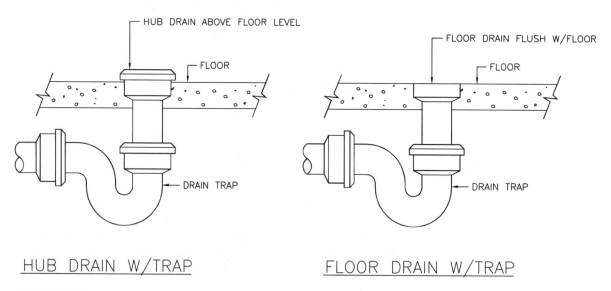

HUB DRAIN ABOVE FLOOR LEVEL

FLOOR

DRAIN TRAP

FLOOR DRAIN FLUSH W/FLOOR

FLOOR

DRAIN TRAP

HUB DRAIN W/TRAP

FLOOR DRAIN W/TRAP

FIGURE 1.87
Floor drains.

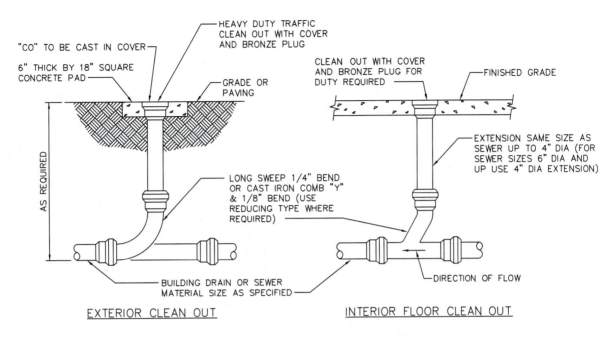

CLEAN OUT EXAMPLES

FIGURE 1.88
Floor clean out.

be located in walls or floors. In the event that a sanitary pipe becomes restricted or clogged, a plumber can use a device known as a snake (see Figure 1.89) to break up the blockage and widen the inside of the pipe.

FIGURE 1.89
Pipe snake.

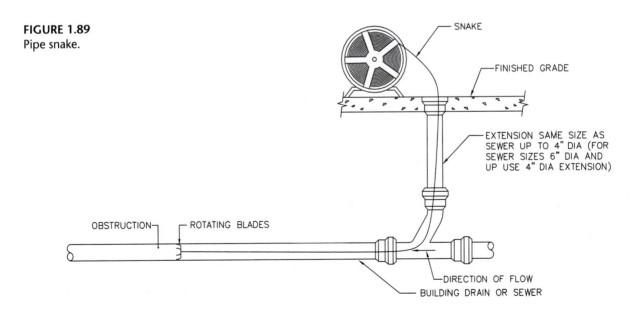

USING A SNAKE

Sanitary waste pipes are among the first items to be installed in a building during new construction. One reason for this is because at least some if not most of the piping installed for use by the lower-level fixtures will be located underground. Because sanitary waste pipes must be installed at an angle, sloping downward away from the fixtures, we must prepare for this consideration by looking at the available space beneath floors under which sanitary pipe must be run. For this reason we try to minimize long horizontal runs of waste pipe between floors. Instead, we utilize short runs of pipe and tie them into a vertical pipe that flows to the level or levels below. The three common horizontal pipe slopes that we will use for the purpose of this text are ⅛-inch fall per foot, ¼-inch fall per foot, and ½-inch fall per foot.

To better understand the concept of pipe slope, let's consider the illustration in Figure 1.90. In this illustration a pipe penetrates a floor slab and begins sloping at 10 ft 6 in. above the finished floor below. The top of the drop ceiling is located 8 ft 10 in. above the same finished floor, which leaves 1 ft 8 in. or 20 in. of vertical space through which the pipe can drop. If we assume that this particular pipe has been sized based upon a ¼-in. fall per foot (meaning that the pipe elevation drops ¼-in. for every foot of horizontal run), we can determine the maximum vertical run of the pipe using the formula:

**horizontal run in feet = allowable drop in inches
÷ pipe fall per foot in inches**

Therefore,

horizontal run = 20 inches ÷ (¼ inch)
horizontal run = **80 feet**

Likewise, if we wanted to know how far this pipe would drop over a run of 60 feet, we would use the following formula:

**fall in inches = (horizontal run in feet)
× (slope per foot in inches)**

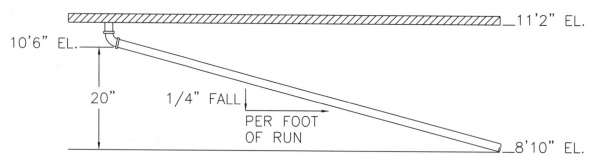

FIGURE 1.90
Example illustration.

Therefore,

$$\text{pipe fall} = 60 \text{ feet} \times (\tfrac{1}{4} \text{ inch})$$
$$\text{pipe fall} = \textbf{15 inches}$$

Figure 1.91 shows a typical small double toilet room layout. Notice how the sanitary waste lines are connected. The short 45° line at each branch represents a wye or double wye (shown in Figure 1.92). In a sanitary waste system, the direction of waste flow is indicated by the direction that the wye turns into the branch or main.

Remember, all of the sanitary pipe is run below the floor level and it is constantly sloping away from the fixtures.

This simple layout has a wall clean out located at the point farthest upstream of the waste flow. There are also two floor drains, one in each toilet room. In order to prevent waste and sediment from drying out in the **trap** of the floor drain, we need to **prime** it. To prime a trap we need to supply a constant flow or regular flow of water to the trap. This serves to flush the trap out and prevent drying. Figure 1.93 shows a typical example of a trap with primer.

FIGURE 1.91
Double toilet room.

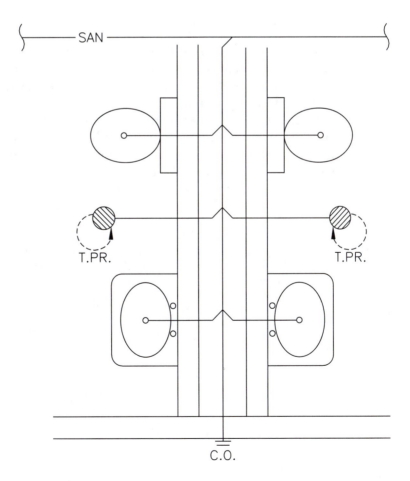

FIGURE 1.92
Wye and double wye.

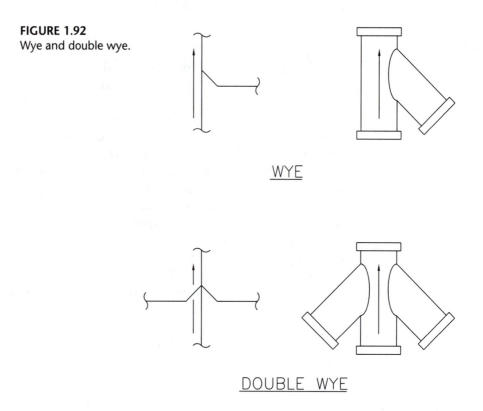

The trap primer line can be connected directly to the trap below floor level, or it can be an above-floor source of water. As long as there is either a constant or regular flow of water to the trap, the trap is considered to be primed.

As mentioned earlier, sanitary waste pipe is used to remove waste from fixtures and floor drains. Additionally, clean outs are placed upstream of flow in locations where pipes need to be accessed for inspection and cleaning. We look next at the sizing of these pipes.

FIGURE 1.93
Trap primer.

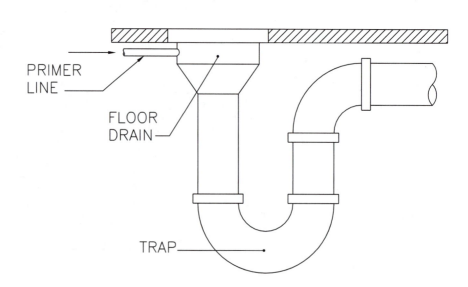

TOPICAL QUESTIONS

Answer the following questions to the best of your ability based on the material covered in this portion of the text. Then check your answers with those found at the end of Part I.

1. What is meant by the term *gravometric?*

2. Describe the placement of a clean out on a sanitary waste line.

3. What are the two purposes of a trap primer?

SIZING SANITARY WASTE PIPING

Sanitary waste piping is sized in a manner that is very similar to domestic water supply pipe sizing. There are, however, two important additional considerations. First, the sizing units are called **drainage fixture units** (DFUs) and are based on a fixture's maximum drain/waste flow requirements. Second, piping in a sanitary waste system is also sized based upon the slope at which it is run.

To investigate this principle, let's take a look at the simple layout in Figure 1.94. Referring to Table 1.5, we find the following DFU values for each of the fixtures in these two rooms: W.C. = 6, LAV = 1. We will assume that the floor drain (F.DR.) is 3 inches: 3 in. F.DR. = 2.

Figure 1.95 shows the layout with all DFU values labeled. Now, looking at Appendix D we see that there are several standard slopes at which drain piping can be run. For simplicity, we will confine the pipe slopes used in this text to ½-inch fall per foot, ¼-inch fall per foot, and ⅛-inch fall per foot. The sizes for the pipes in this example are shown for ¼-inch fall per foot in Figure 1.95 A and for ½-inch fall per foot in Figure 1.95 B.

Notice in Figure 1.95 that some of the sizes have been circled. Although these are the appropriate sizes for flow demand found in Appendix D for these particular pipes, we have resized these pipes for the two following reasons: (1) All water closets require a minimum 3-inch drain; and (2) it is common practice to maintain pipe sizes and avoid reductions wherever possible.

Now, let's look at a more complex application of these principles in a small two-story building.

TABLE 1.5   DRAINAGE FIXTURE UNITS FOR FIXTURES AND GROUPS

FIXTURE TYPE	DRAINAGE FIXTURE UNIT VALUE AS LOAD FACTORS	MINIMUM SIZE OF TRAP (inches)
Bathroom group consisting of water closet, lavatory, bidet and bathtub or shower	6	—
Bathtub[a] (with or without overhead shower or whirlpool attachments)	2	$1\frac{1}{2}$
Bidet	2	$1\frac{1}{4}$
Combination sink and tray	2	$1\frac{1}{2}$
Dental unit or cuspidor	1	$1\frac{1}{4}$
Dental lavatory	1	$1\frac{1}{4}$
Drinking fountain	$\frac{1}{2}$	$1\frac{1}{4}$
Dishwashing machine,[b] domestic	2	$1\frac{1}{2}$
Floor drains	2	2
Kitchen sink, domestic	2	$1\frac{1}{2}$
Kitchen sink, domestic with food waste grinder and/or dishwasher	2	$1\frac{1}{2}$
Lavatory	1	$1\frac{1}{4}$
Laundry tray (1 or 2 compartments)	2	$1\frac{1}{2}$
Shower compartment, domestic	2	2
Sinks		
Surgeon's	3	$1\frac{1}{2}$
Flushing rim (with valve)	6	3
Service (trap standard)	3	3
Service ("P" trap)	2	2
Pot, scullery, etc.[b]	4	$1\frac{1}{2}$
Urinal, pedestal, siphon jet, blowout	6	Footnote d
Urinal, wall lip	4	Footnote d
Urinal, washout	4	Footnote d
Washing machines, commercial[c]	3	2
Washing machine, residential	2	2
Wash sink (circular or multiple) each set of faucets	2	$1\frac{1}{2}$
Water closet, flushometer tank, public or private	4[e]	Footnote d
Water closet, private installation	4	Footnote d
Water closet, public installation	6	Footnote d

For **SI:** 1 inch = 25.4 mm.

b A showerhead over a bathtub or whirlpool bathtub attachments does not increase the drainage fixture unit value.

d Trap size shall be consistent with the fixture outlet size.

e For the purpose of computing loads on building drains and sewers, water closets or urinals shall not be rated at a lower drainage fixture unit unless the lower values are confirmed by testing.

Source: Courtesy of International Code Council. Reprinted from International Plumbing Code 1997 with permission.

FIGURE 1.94
Double toilet room with
DFU labels.

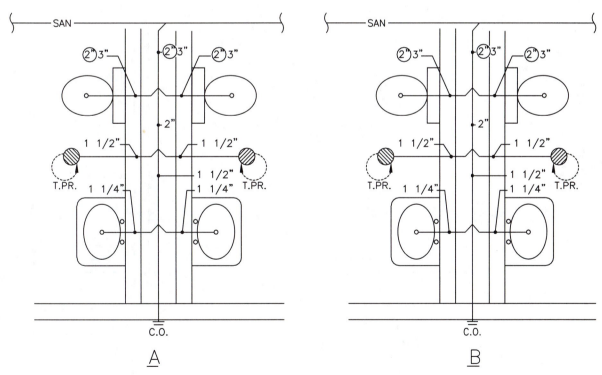

FIGURE 1.95
Double toilet room with pipe sizes.

Example   **3.1**

Figure 1.96 shows a small two-story building with sanitary waste pipe. The appropriate DFU values have been assigned to each fixture from Table 1.5. First, all lines serving the W.C.s must be a minimum 3 inches. Therefore, we'll assign these sizes. All other sizes will not differ whether the pipe fall is ¼ inch per foot or ½ inch per foot because the total DFU value of 16.5 does not exceed 21 (the values at which the pipe sizes begin to diverge). Figure 1.97 shows all DFU assignments and pipe sizes from Appendix D. Those sizes that have been altered are circled with the new pipe size shown alongside each; for example, all piping downstream of the water closets on each floor are resized to 3 inches for **IPC** code as discussed previously. On the first floor, 2 inches was chosen for the line size for the clean out (C.O.) because it is easier to change pipe size from 2 inches to 3 inches than 1½ inches to 3 inches. On the second floor the sanitary main is maintained at 3 inches at its upstream end to eliminate an extra reducing fitting for a very short run of smaller pipe.

FIGURE 1.96
Simple two-story
sanitary layout.

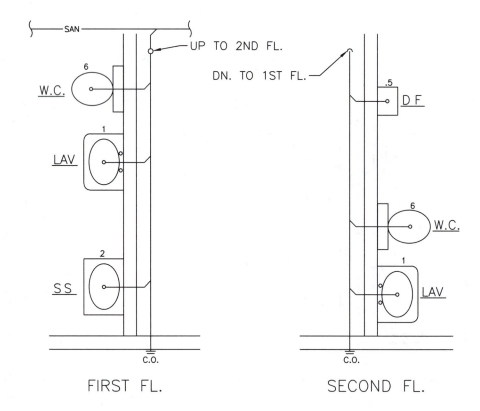

FIRST FL.   SECOND FL.

FIGURE 1.97
Sample two-story sanitary layout with sizes.

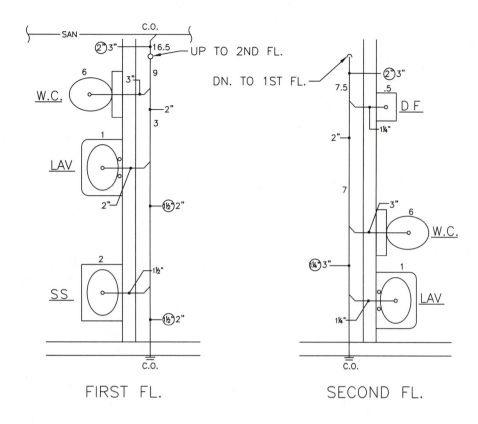

FIRST FL.   SECOND FL.

Sample Problem   3.1

A certain sanitary main runs 100 feet through an 18-inch-high crawl space. If this pipe is designed to service 63 DFU, what is the minimum required pipe size? Rewriting the previous formula:

$$Slope/ft = Fall(in.) \div Run(ft)$$
$$Slope/ft = 18 \text{ in.} \div 100 \text{ ft} = .18 \text{ in./ft}$$
$$0.125 < 0.18 < 0.25$$

Therefore, standard fall to be used equals ⅛ inch per foot. Using Appendix D we find 63 DFU at ⅛ inch fall per foot yields a **4-inch pipe.**

Sample Problem   3.2

A sanitary main running at a slope of ¼-inch per fall per foot services the following fixtures in order from its end moving downstream: 2 bathroom groups, 2 floor drains, 2 drinking fountains, 1 urinal, 1 lavatory sink. (a) Draw a simple sketch of this layout. (b) Determine the size of the main only between each branch. (c) Recommend a C.O. size for this line.

FIGURE 1.98
Sample problem sketch.

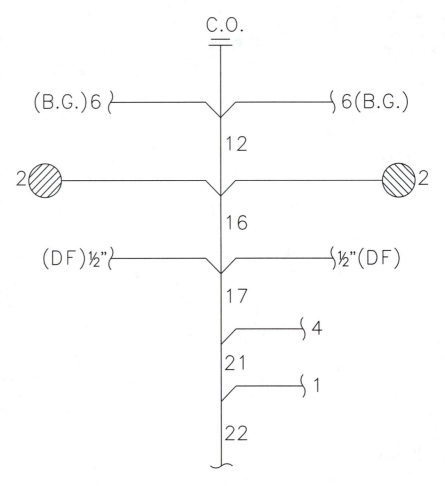

(a) Figure 1.98 shows a sample sketch with DFU values assigned. (b) The entire run of pipe, except for the segment from the clean out, services at least 1 W.C. This automatically makes the minimum size 3 inches. Because 22 DFU at ¼-inch fall = 72½-inch pipe, we need to use a 3-inch pipe for all segments. (c) C.O. = 3 inches, because the entire line is 3 inches.

Sample Problem   3.3

A certain sanitary pipe runs horizontally in a ceiling space that is 3 ft 2 in. deep. The steel joists supporting the floor above are 18-in. deep. If all pipe must run under the joists, and the horizontal pipe run is 100 ft, what size must the pipe be to service 121 DFU adequately?

SANITARY WASTE VENT SYSTEM DESIGN AND APPLICATIONS

The purpose of a **sanitary waste vent system** is to:

1. Prevent **siphonage (backflow)** of waste by balancing the sanitary waste line pressure with the **ambient** atmospheric pressure.

2. Allow a means of escape for lighter-than-air gases generated in waste pipe.

Siphonage occurs in closed waste pipe systems due to two related phenomena: the **Bernoulli principle** and the **Venturi effect.**

The *Bernoulli principle* states that the air pressure perpendicular to a moving surface will decrease as the velocity of that surface increases. Therefore, as waste travels more quickly down a soil pipe, it reduces the air pressure along its path, creating a partial vacuum in the pipe.

The *Venturi effect* is a direct result of the vacuum created by the Bernoulli principle. This effect causes material to rush into the pipe in areas where partial vacuums have formed as a result of the Bernoulli principle. When no matter, such as air, is available to fill the vacuum, waste material from within the pipe itself will flow back into the space causing a condition known as *backflow*. If the backflow momentum is great enough, the waste material will be ejected through fixtures and drains connected to the waste line.

Vent systems are made up of three components as shown in Figure 1.99.

Soil Stack — Vertical runoff **vent pipe** connecting directly to a fixture or sanitary line.

Tie-In — Horizontal runs and connections that join stacks to the VTR.

VTR — Vent through roof. This is the highest vertical run of pipe. It penetrates the roof to access air outside the building. A rule of thumb, based on IPC 1997, states that the maximum amount of vent pipe that may be run horizontally in any group of pipe is approximately 90%. This is very important because the air will not move as freely through a combination of horizontal and vertical pipe as it will through a straight run of pipe.

Notice that all vent tie-ins are made using 45° elbows instead of 90° elbows. This allows the air to move more easily through the pipes.

Figure 1.100 shows a typical sanitary vent piping plan for a pair of toilet rooms.

Notice how all of the vent piping (shown in dashed lines) starts from a point along the sanitary line. The VTR is located where the full circle appears, indicating that this pipe continues to go up through the next level.

Next we discuss how to size these vent pipes.

FIGURE 1.99
Vent stack and tie-in.

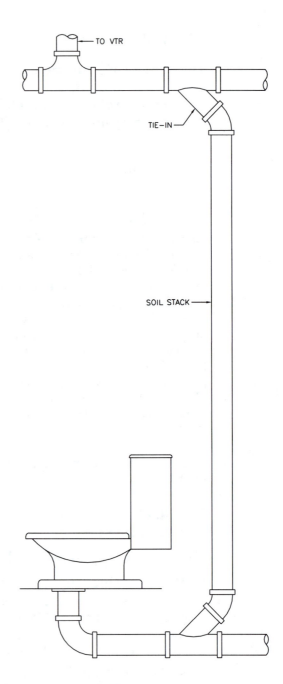

TOPICAL QUESTIONS

Answer the following questions to the best of your ability based on the material covered in this portion of the text. Then check your answers with those found at the end of Part I.

FIGURE 1.100
Double toilet room with vent piping.

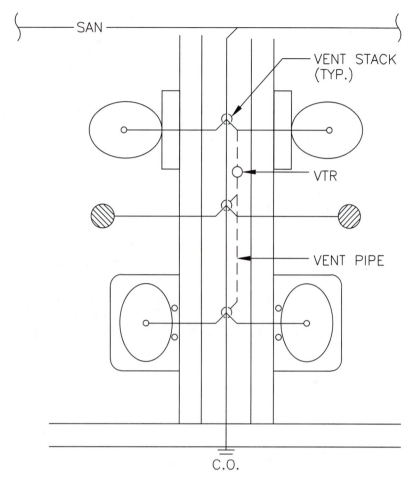

1. Name the two purposes for a sanitary waste vent system.

2. Where do you think that the horizontal runs of vent piping are located?

3. At what angle do vent stacks attach to horizontal vent pipes?

SIZING SANITARY WASTE VENT PIPING

The sizing of waste vent piping is relatively easy. All we really need to know about a vent pipe to size it correctly are (1) the total DFUs serviced, (2) the stack diameter (based on fixture DFU rating), and (3) the **developed length** in feet of the vent run. By developed length what we mean is the total length of pipe needed to run from the fixture vent connection to the *VTR*.

Let's consider as an example, a public water closet with a single vent through the roof. The roof level is 12 feet above the W.C. vent connection. Using Appendix D, we find that a 6 DFU fixture requires a 1½-inch soil pipe. Because there are no bends or tie-ins, we can leave the overall size at 1½ inches.

Notice in Appendix E that the diameter of vent pipe based on developed length never exceeds the corresponding soil stack diameter based on DFU.

Now, let's look at a more complex application of vent piping. Figure 1.101 shows a series of four toilet rooms located along a corridor in close proximity to one another. An important item to note here is that all horizontal pipe on a sanitary vent plan is run in the ceiling space above the floor unless otherwise noted. For this example we'll assume that the ceiling space is 10 feet above the floor, and the VTR penetrates the roof 6½ feet above the ceiling. Figure 1.102 shows a typical elevation view of this layout with dimensions included. The circled numbers indicate the total DFUs serviced by each branch.

To size each stack we simply use Appendix E to find the corresponding pipe size for the DFU rating indicated.

Fixture	DFU	Stack
LAV	1	1¼ in.
F.DR.	2	1¼ in.
W.C.	6	1¼ in.

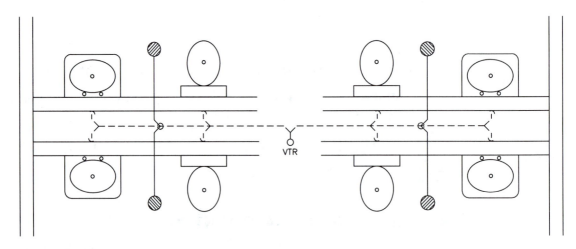

FIGURE 1.101
Four rest rooms.

FIGURE 1.102
Rest room part
elevation.

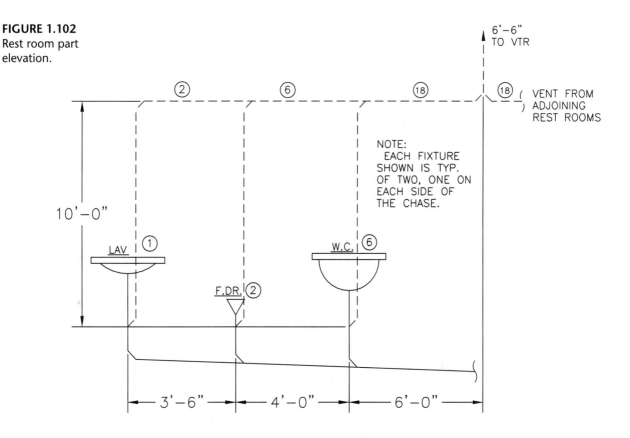

To size each branch of the tie-ins, we need to look at the total DFUs serviced at each and the length of the pipe from fixture to VTR. A simple chart of these values yields the following:

Branch DFU	Developed Length	Size
2	30 ft	1¼ in.
6	26 ft-6 in.	1⅛ in.
18	22 ft-6 in.	2 in.
36	stack only	3 in.

The venting plan with indicated sizes is shown in Figure 1.103. Now, let's look at some sample problems that use this sizing procedure.

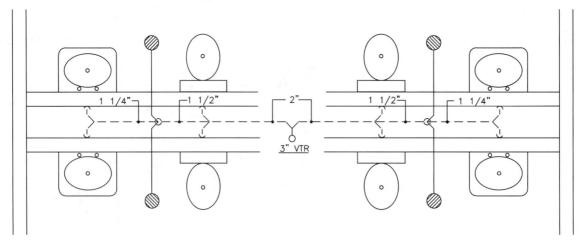

FIGURE 1.103
Four rest rooms with sizes.

Sample Problem   3.4

Six public water closets are placed in a rest room 4 feet apart on center. These six water closets all vent to the same VTR located 20 feet from the last toilet in-line with the others. The ceiling space is located 9 feet A.F.F. (above finished floor) and the roof is 17 feet A.F.F. Draw a complete plan and elevation sketch of this scenario. Include all dimensions and DFU ratings.

Solution:

See Figure 1.104.

Sample Problem   3.5

Using the sketches you developed in Sample Problem 3.4, determine the size of each stack and tie-in. Use a chart similar to the one shown previously to determine the size of all horizontal piping.

Solution:

Each water closet will require a 1½-inch stack according to Appendix E.

Branch DFU	Developed Length	Size
6	57 ft	1½ in.
12	53 ft	1½ in.
18	49 ft	1½ in.
24	45 ft	2 in.
30	41 ft	2 in.
36	37 ft	2 in.

Figure 1.105 shows the floor plan with vent sizes labeled.

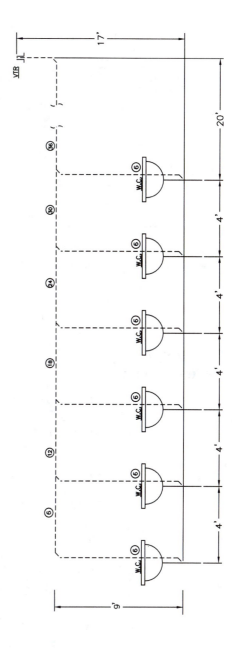

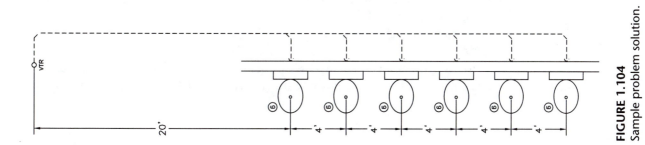

FIGURE 1.104
Sample problem solution.

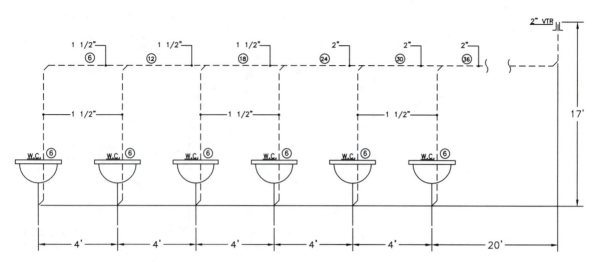

FIGURE 1.105
Elevation view with vent sizes.

Sample Problem   3.6

What size VTR would you recommend for a vent system servicing a total of 125 DFU if the closest fixture to the VTR is 68 feet away from it along the path of the vent pipe?

SANITARY WASTE AND VENT PLUMBING PLANS

In this section we take a brief look at a pair of rest rooms showing both waste and vent lines. It is customary to show both of these systems on a **sanitary plan,** just as it is customary to show both hot and cold water systems on a domestic water plumbing plan.

Referring to Figure 1.106 we see a typical men's and women's rest room combination. Notice how all of the branches and tie-ins of both the waste and vent pipes are connected using 45° angled lines. These lines represent wye fittings, and the direction in which these fittings are angled indicates the direction of waste flow or the direction from the fixture to the VTR.

Notice how the vent stacks are shown connecting to the sanitary waste line in the common chase and along each outer rest room wall. Because plumbing plans are schematic in nature, we have the liberty of relocating pipes on the drawing to avoid cluttering. The vent pipes

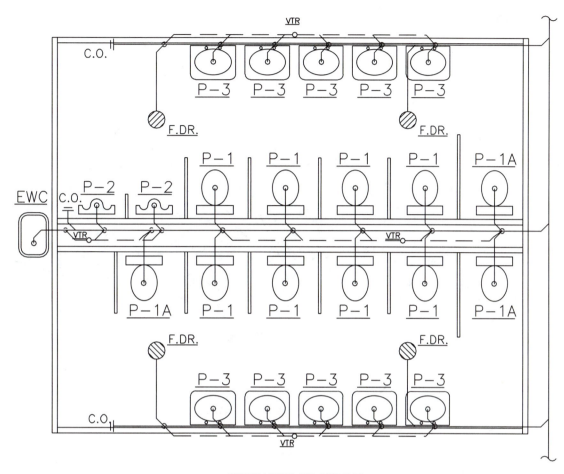

SANITARY WASTE AND VENT PLAN

FIGURE 1.106
Men's and women's room combination
with common wall chase.

located behind each row of lavatory sinks are not actually located outside the wall spaces, but are shown as such for clarity on the plan.

Figure 1.107 shows the same plan with the piping in isometric
view. From this view we can see that the pipes venting each fixture
are attached to the sanitary drain lines inside the walls or chases. We
can also see that the vent pipes serving the floor drain lines are
attached where the drain pipe enters the chase. This figure is a typical
isometric sanitary riser diagram. Now, let's look at the procedure for
generating a standard sanitary riser diagram.

FIGURE 1.107
Sanitary isometric
diagram.

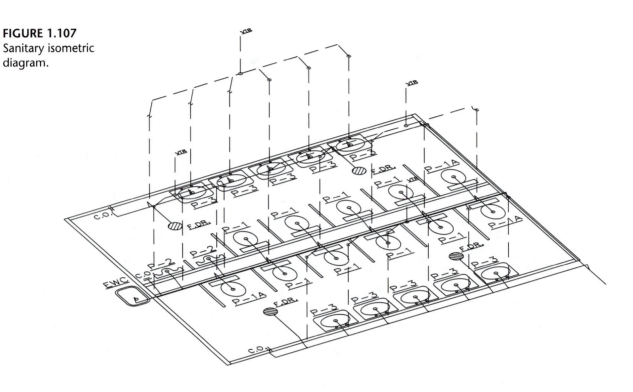

SANITARY WASTE AND VENT ISOMETRIC RISER DIAGRAM

TOPICAL QUESTIONS

Answer the following questions to the best of your ability based on the material covered in this portion of the text. Then check your answers with those found at the end of Part I.

1. Briefly describe a sanitary waste plan.

2. How is the direction of waste flow indicated on a sanitary plan?

3. What added condition might be of concern when running a sanitary pipe horizontally through a ceiling space?

SANITARY WASTE AND VENT RISER DIAGRAMS

In this final section of Part I, we continue to take a look at Figure 1.106. We use this diagram to develop a sanitary waste and vent riser diagram. Figure 1.108 illustrates the sanitary waste and vent riser diagram for Figure 1.106. The development of this type of riser diagram is similar to the development of a domestic water riser diagram.

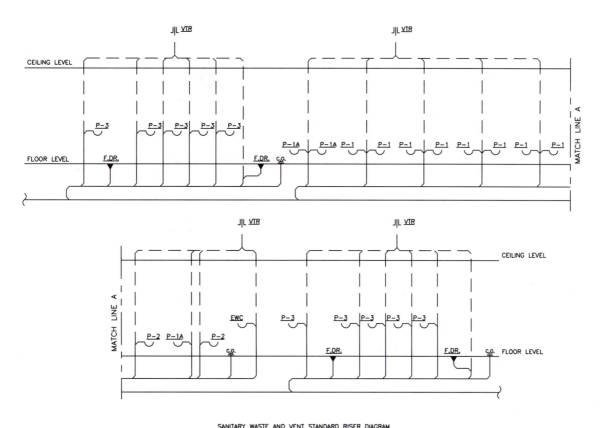

FIGURE 1.108
Sanitary waste and vent riser diagram.

The main difference is that the waste and vent riser diagram represents the avenues through which materials are carried away from the plumbing fixtures. This is, of course, with the exception that the vent piping also allows air to enter the system to prevent the siphonage of waste materials.

Using the same procedure that we used previously to describe the generation of domestic water, we'll trace the development of this riser diagram. Referring to Figure 1.109, we see that the sanitary waste and vent lines for the men's room lavatory sinks and floor drains have been highlighted. Looking at the floor plan in the lower left of Figure 1.109, we can see that the wyes are angled toward the downstream direction of the sanitary main. The downstream end of a sanitary line is the best place to begin a riser diagram.

Following the highlighted portion of this figure, let's move upstream toward the fixtures. When laying out sanitary waste riser diagrams, we always move upstream toward the fixtures. Using this method, we can determine whether each branch of the riser diagram turns to the right or left. Moving upstream in this diagram we need to

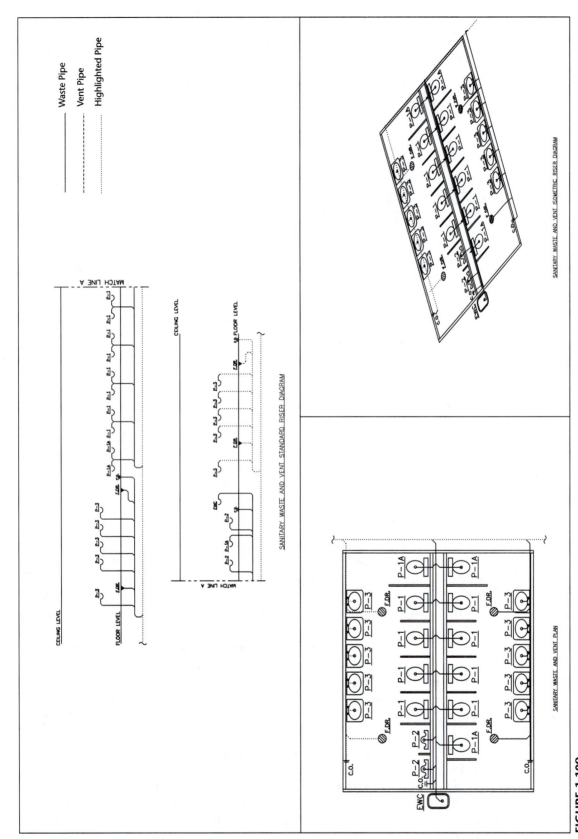

FIGURE 1.109
Sanitary diagrams.

turn to the right to move toward the lavatory sinks in the men's room. Notice that the highlighted sanitary line branch turns to the right on the standard riser diagram; however, the tie-in to the sanitary main is angled first to the left. This is because all tie-ins must be angled in the direction of waste flow. Each sink is located to the left of its respective tie-in on the riser diagram, indicating that each sink is located to the left of the branch as we move upstream. The floor drains and clean outs are also located in proper sequence.

Figure 1.110 highlights the portion of this sanitary waste system that services the toilets and urinals in the men's room. This figure also shows the run out to the water cooler located at the end of the common chase. Notice that the branch turns again to the right off the main (this occurs in the upper portion of the riser diagram to the left of match line A).

Notice that all of the toilets that face to the right on the riser diagram have been highlighted. This particular branch crosses the **match line**. In instances where the riser diagram becomes too long to fit on a single drawing, it is often broken into two or more parts, which are stacked on the same page.

Moving along this same branch, the nonhighlighted toilets are those located in the women's rest room. The remaining lavatory sinks, floor drains, and clean outs are shown in the far upper left of the riser.

Once the sanitary waste lines have been drawn on the riser, adding the vent piping is relatively simple. Wherever the vent line is shown as dropping into the sanitary pipe at a fixture, we place a vertical dashed line (see Figure 1.111). Notice that two of the floor drains are not shown with vent stacks on the riser. These two drains have no direct venting on the floor plan because they are located very close to two sinks that are being vented. By slightly oversizing one or both of these vent stacks, we can account for the demand of each drain.

Figure 1.112 shows the completed waste and vent riser diagram. Notice that the tie-ins to the horizontal vents are all angled toward each VTR. Also, the VTRs have been located at or between the same fixtures on the riser as they are located on the plumbing plan.

As with domestic water riser diagrams, it is customary to show pipe sizes on the sanitary riser as well. However, unlike domestic water risers, sanitary risers do not require the use of direction arrows.

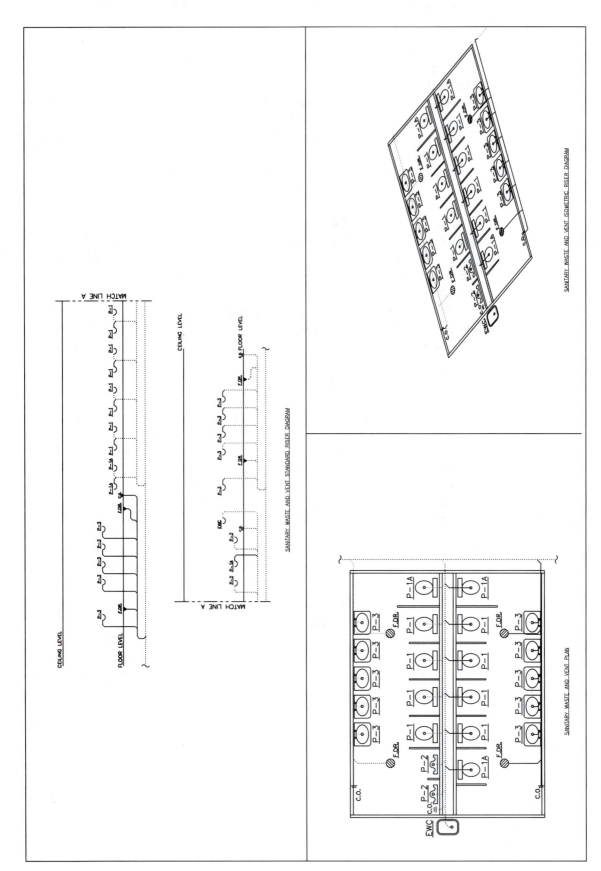

FIGURE 1.110
Sanitary diagrams.

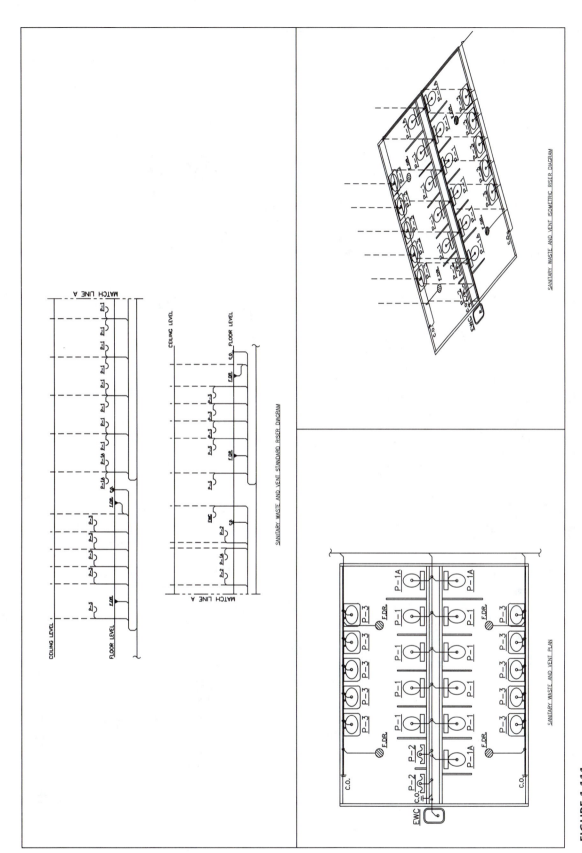

FIGURE 1.111
Sanitary diagrams with vent stacks.

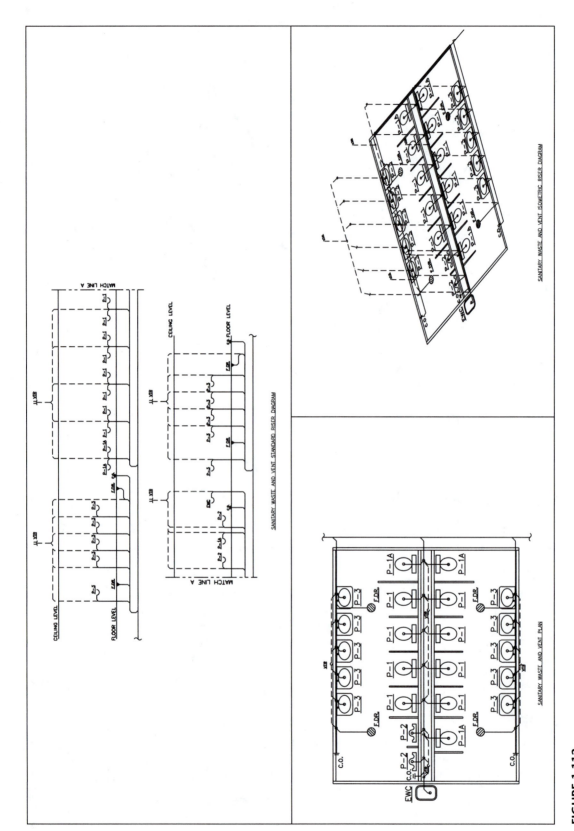

FIGURE 1.112
Complete sanitary vent diagram.

TOPICAL QUESTIONS

Answer the following questions to the best of your ability based on the material covered in this portion of the text. Then check your answers with those found at the end of Part I.

1. Where is the best place to begin drawing a sanitary waste and vent riser diagram?

2. What drafting symbol can be used when a riser diagram becomes too long to fit on a single page?

3. What symbols that commonly appear on a domestic water riser diagram are not necessary to show on a sanitary riser?

ANSWERS TO PART I QUESTIONS AND PROBLEMS

Pipes

1. Pipes are metal or plastic tubes used to direct fluid flow in a plumbing system.

2. (a) solder, (b) thread, (c) butt-weld.

3. In sanitary waste and storm water systems.

Valves

1. To regulate fluid flow.

2. (a) to stop flow at a fixture, (b) to prevent backflow into a tank or pump, (c) to reduce line pressure for use in a system, (d) to regulate pressure inside a boiler or hot water heater.

3. To reduce the water pressure from a public utility line so that it can safely service a home or building.

Fittings

1. (a) to connect two pipes, (b) to change the direction of piping, (c) to change the size of piping.

2. (a) couplings, unions, and flanges; (b) elbows, tees, wyes, and crosses; (c) reducers, bushings, reducing fittings.

3. 90° elbow, tee, cross (weld-o-lets and thread-o-lets may also serve this purpose).

Fixtures

1. To utilize the water supplied by the plumbing system.

2. Water closet, urinal, drinking fountain, water cooler, hose bibb.

3. A flush valve fixture operates under pressure from the water supply and requires a higher supply flow rate.

Building Inlet Supply and Regulation Systems

1. Water that is suitable for human comsumption and/or contact.

2. Pressure may be increased by means of a pump, decreased by valving, or balanced by a combination of pumps and valving.

3. For delivery to a drinking fountain or as a supply to cooling coils in a conditioned ventilation system.

Cold Water Supply and Applications

1. Chilled water systems are maintained at a lower temperature by refrigeration whereas cold water systems often operate at or near underground temperature levels.

2. To provide an opening in the architecture through which elements of a system can pass. HVAC, plumbing, and electrical.

3. A supply that is provided from a source or off a main to a specific area of a building.

Hot Water Heating Systems

1. Tempered water ranges from 85°F to 120°F, while hot water is over 120°F.

2. Electricity, propane, natural gas, coal, oil.

3. In case the pressure relief valve actuates or in the event that the heater must be drained for maintenance.

Hot Water Supply Design and Applications

1. Because usually fewer appliances and fixtures require hot water than require cold water.

2. Recirculation.

3. A mixing valve.

Sample Problem 2.3

(a) DF—¾-in, W.C.—1½-in., UR—1½-in., LAV—½-in., SS—¾-in.; (b) see sketch Figure 1.113; (c) 16 wsfu (round up from 15.25 wsfu) = 18.0 gpm.

FIGURE 1.113

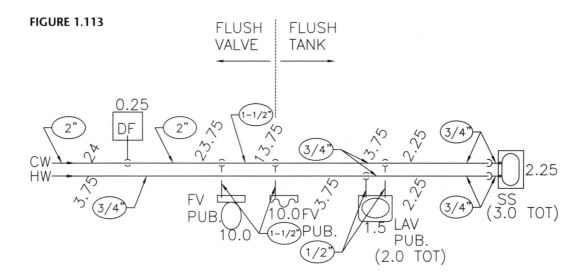

Sample Problem 2.6

6 gpm.

Domestic Water Plumbing Plans

1. A standard architectural floor plan background with a single-line piping schematic superimposed upon it.

2. In a plumbing symbols legend.

3. A letter/number designation assigned to each type of fixture (e.g. P-1 may represent a water closet).

Domestic Water Riser Diagrams

1. To provide a "road map" that shows the order in which the water supply pathways occur.

2. A standard riser is a "flat" diagram; an isometric riser is a 3-D type of wire frame.

3. Because there is more room and less clutter on the riser.

Miscellaneous Considerations

1. Prevent heat transfer and retard condensation.

2. When the pipe is insulated or when the pipe material is too soft to support its own weight.

3. (a) hot water or steam pipes, (b) long runs of straight pipe, (c) multiple pipes running horizontally parallel.

Sanitary Waste System Design and Applications

1. Operating under the force of gravity.

2. It is located in an accessible area and attaches to the end of a waste pipe in the direction opposite of flow.

3. To flush a trap and to keep it moist.

Sample Problem 3.3

4 inches (using Appendix D based on ¼-inch fall per foot)

Sanitary Waste Vent System Design and Applications

1. To prevent siphonage and to allow gases to escape.

2. In the ceiling space above the fixtures.

3. 45 degrees.

Sample Problem 3.6

3 in.

Sanitary Waste and Vent Plumbing Plans

1. A standard architectural floor plan background with single-line sanitary and vent piping schematics superimposed upon it.

2. By the angle of the wyes connecting the branches to the main.

3. All horizontal sanitary pipe runs have slope. This limits the distance they can run through a restricted space.

Sanitary Waste and Vent Riser Diagrams

1. At the farthest point downstream on the main.

2. A match line.

3. Direction arrows.

PART II

Application Problems

SECTION 1

Domestic Water Systems

1. Water flows into a holding tank from a large pipe. If the holding tank has a capacity of 76,000 gallons and the supply pipe can provide enough water to fill the tank in 12 hours, what is the flow rate (in gpm) of the water through the supply pipe?

2. If the tank in problem 1 supplies a small community that has a peak demand of 10,000 gph (gallons per hour), what will the volume of water be in the tank after 3 hours if the demand begins when the tank is full? Assume that water is constantly delivered to the tank through the supply pipe during this time.

3. How long will it take to fill a 150-gallon tub with water if the tub is supplied with water using a 2-inch copper pipe at maximum flow capacity? (Assume a 4 psi per 100 ft pressure drop in a predominantly flush tank system.)

4. A certain pipe has an inside diameter of ¾ of an inch. Water passes from one end of this pipe to the other end in 15 seconds at a flow rate of 5 gpm. How long is this pipe?

5. A cold water main services the following fixtures in order moving downstream: two public lavatory sinks, one public flush valve urinal, three public flush valve toilets, and one mop sink. Assuming all take-offs are perpendicular to the main and further assuming that the remaining demand downstream of the mop sink is 30 gpm, determine the size of each segment of the CW main.

6. A certain hot water main services 16 public and 4 private lavatory sinks. Additionally, the same main services 4 private shower/tub combinations. Using a continuous loop determine the size of a 30% HWC line for this system.

7. If the line in problem 6 services the public lavatories from one branch and the remaining private fixture from another branch, determine the size for a 20% HWC line for each branch.

8. Sketch a standard and an isometric riser diagram for the plumbing part plan shown in Figure 2.1.

9. Water weighs 62.4 pounds per cubic foot. If a vertical line is tapped from a supply main having a line pressure of 40 psi, how high must the line run before water will no longer run out from the top?

10. What will be the size and material needed for a cold water main that services a system with a 250 gpm demand if the system is predominantly (a) flush tank, (b) flush valve?

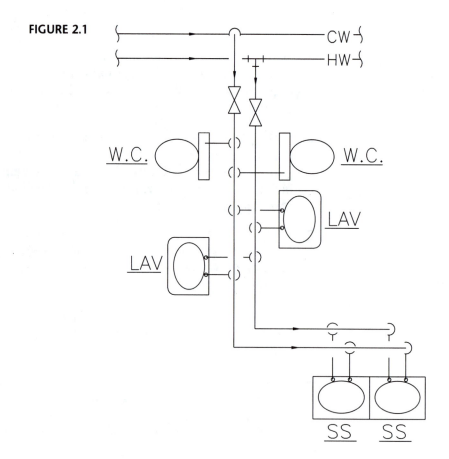

FIGURE 2.1

PART PLAN

SECTION 2

Sanitary Waste and Vent Systems

1. A sanitary waste pipe has an O.D. of 6 inches. How far can this pipe run horizontally if it slopes at ¼-inch per foot through a vertical clearance of 26 inches?

2. How far can the pipe in problem 1 run horizontally if its centerline begins 26 inches above the bottom vertical clearance level?

3. A pipe can slope a maximum of 14 inches along a horizontal distance of 50 feet. What is the minimum pipe size required to service 125 DFU along this run?

4. Seven fixtures tie into a sanitary main moving downstream in the following order: a drinking fountain, a pair of flush valve water closets (connected with a double wye), an additional flush valve water closet and urinal (combined with double wye), and a pair of lavatory sinks (also connected with a double wye). Determine the size of the main between each fixture or pair of fixtures.

5. Recommend sizes for each sanitary pipe branch in problem 4. Also recommend floor drain and C.O. sizes to tie in to the main.

6. Sketch the layout described in problems 4 and 5. Show soil vent stack tie-ins and sizes. Also, determine the size VTR needed for this group of fixtures.

7. Sketch a complete standard sanitary waste and vent riser diagram for the layout in problem 6.

8. A public arena has a pair of rest rooms located 345 feet away from a tie-in to the sanitary main. Each rest room contains 34 W.C., 16 lavatory sinks, and one mop sink. Allowing for an additional 18-inch verti-

cal pipe drop, how far below these rest rooms should the sanitary main be located based on (a) ¼-inch fall/ft? (b) ⅛-inch fall/ft?

9. Determine the size for the pipes described in problems 8a and 8b.

10. What is the minimum number of VTRs needed to service the total quantity of fixtures in both rest rooms described in problem 8?

SOLUTIONS TO PART II PROBLEMS

Section 1

1. 76,000 gal/12 hr = 6333 1/3 gal/hr = **105.56 gpm**

2.   supply = 6333.33 gal/hr × 3hrs = +19,000 gal

    demand = 10,000 gal/hr × 3hrs = $\underline{-30,000\ \text{gal}}$

                                        $-11,000$ gal

    vol = 76,000 gal (cap) − 11,000 gal = **65,000 gal**

3. 2-in. pipe @ −4 psi/100 ft = (Appendix C) 70 gpm

    time = 150 gal/70 gpm = **2.14 min** or **2 min 9 sec**

4. V_{15} = (5 ~~gal/min~~) × (1 ~~min~~/60 ~~sec~~) × (15~~sec~~) × (231 in.^{3}/~~gal~~)

    V_{15} = 288 in.^{3} (in 15 sec)

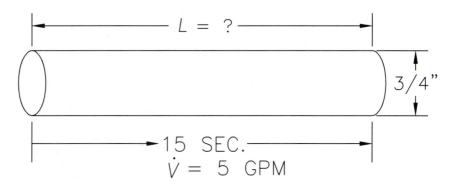

FIGURE 2.2

$V = \frac{1}{4}\pi d^2 l = l = 4V/\pi d^2 = 653.93$ in. = **54.49 ft** (See Figure 2.2.)

5. To find equivalent wsfu @ 30 gpm:

50	29.1	(by interpolation)
x	30	
60	32.0	

    $(30 − 29.1)/(32.0 − 29.1) × (60 − 50) = 3.10$

    wsfu = 50 + 3.10 = 53.10 (round to 53 wsfu)

FIGURE 2.3

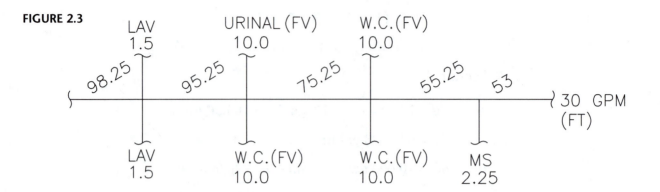

NOTE: ALL FIXTURES SHOWN ARE PUBLIC FIXTURES.

One possible solution based on Figure 2.3 and the value above is:

wsfu	fv/ft	size
53	ft	1½ in.
55.25	fv	2 in.
75.25	fv	2 in.
95.25	fv	2 in.
98.25	fv	2 in.

6. LAV (public): 16×1.5 = 24 wsfu

   LAV (private): 4×0.5 = 2 wsfu

   shower/tub (private): 4×2.25 = 9 wsfu (combination fixture)

   _____

   35 wsfu

   30% of 24.9 gpm (equal to 35 wsfu) = 7.47 gpm = 4 pfu

   yields: ¾ **in. HWC** (Appendix B) or **1 in. HWC** (Appendix C)

7. Interpolating for 24 wsfu: 20   19.6

                                 24   x

                                 25   21.5

   $4/5 \times (21.5 - 19.6) + 19.6 = 21.12$ gpm

   a. total public: 24 wsfu = 21.12 gpm $\times$ 20% = 4.22 gpm

      size: ¾ **in.** (Appendix C)

   b. total private: 11 wsfu = 15.4 gpm $\times$ 20% = 3.08

      size: ⅝ **in.** or ¾ **in.** (Appendix C)

8.

FIGURE 2.4

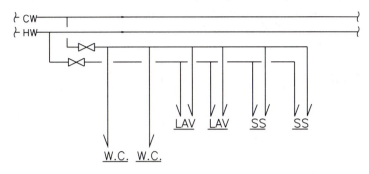

STANDARD RISER DIAGRAM

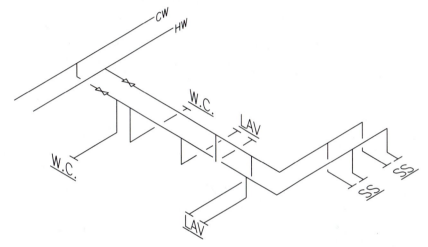

ISOMETRIC RISER DIAGRAM

9. Use a 1 in. $\times$ 1 in. water column. Determine how tall the column will be when it contains 40 lb of water.

FIGURE 2.5

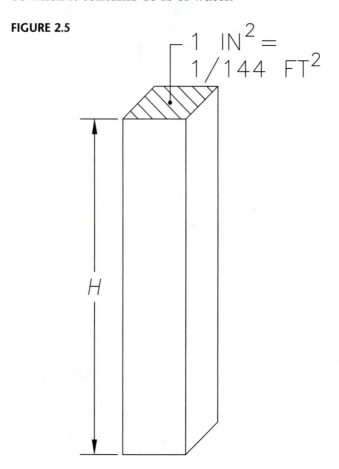

$$V_{REQ'D} = 40 \text{ lb} / (62.4 \text{ lb/ft}^3) = 0.641 \text{ ft3} = 1107.69 \text{ in.}^3$$

$$h = V/A = 1107.69 \text{ in.}^3/1 \text{ in.}^2 = \textbf{1107.69 in.} \text{ or } \textbf{92.31 ft}$$

10. 250 gpm

ft = **2 in. copper** or fv = **3 in. steel** (Appendix B)

Section 2

1. Total run = 26 in. ÷ (¼-in. fall per foot) = **104 ft** (See Figure 2.6.)

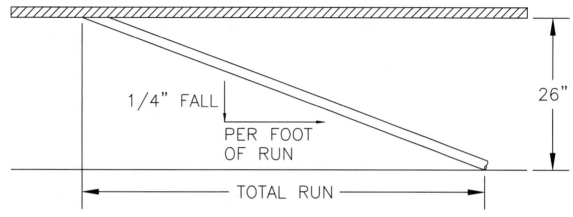

FIGURE 2.6

2. Total run = (26 in. - 3 in.) ÷ (¼-in. fall per foot) = **92 ft** (See Figure 2.7.)

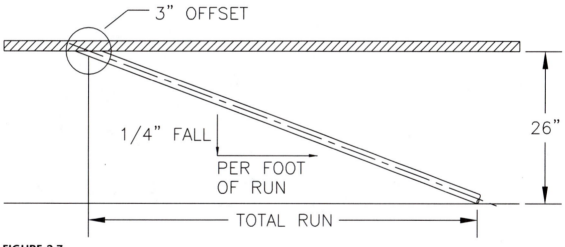

FIGURE 2.7

3. Slope: 14 in./50 ft = 0.28 in./ft ≈ ¼-in. fall per foot

    pipe size: **4 in.** (Appendix D)

4. Refer to Figure 2.8 for branch DFU ratings.

	0.5 DFU	12.5 DFU	22.5 DFU	24.5 DFU
⅛-in. fall/ft	3 in.	3 in.	3 in.	3 in.
¼-in. fall/ft	1¼ in.	2 in.	2½ in.	3 in.
½-in. fall/ft	1¼ in.	2 in.	2½ in.	2½ in.

FIGURE 2.8

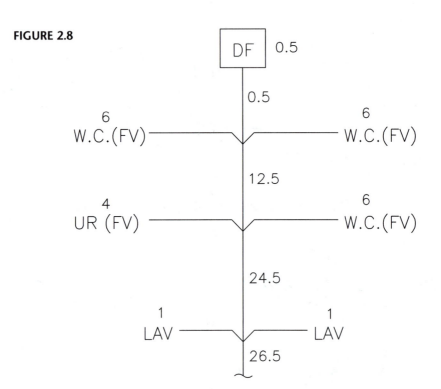

5. All branch sizes shown in Figure 2.9 are based on ¼-in. fall/ft.

FIGURE 2.9

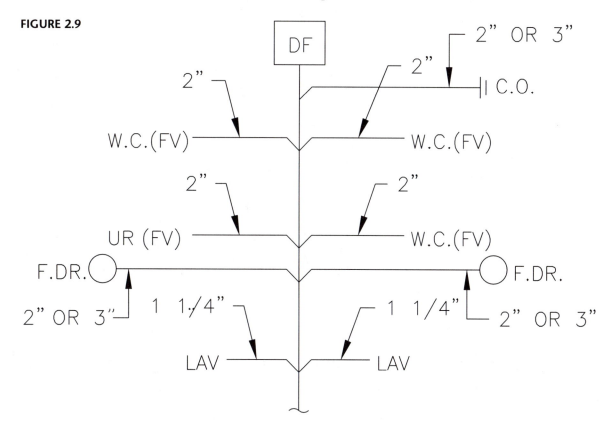

6. Total DFU*:

lavatory sinks:	2 @ 1 DFU ea	= 2 DFU
water closets:	3 @ 6 DFU ea	= 18 DFU
urinal:	1 @ 4 DFU ea	= 4 DFU
drinking fountain:	1 @ ½ DFU ea	= 0.5 DFU
		24.5 dfu

VTR size: **1½-in.** (Appendix E) (See Figure 2.10 for the part plan.)

*Highest values for fixture DFUs were used from Table 1.5.

FIGURE 2.10

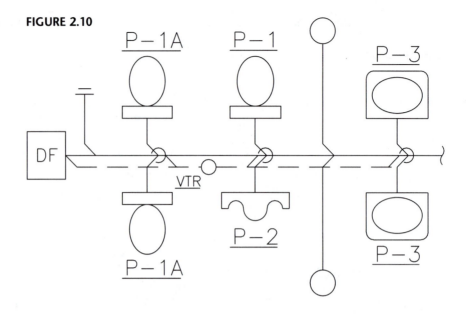

7. Refer to Figure 2.11.

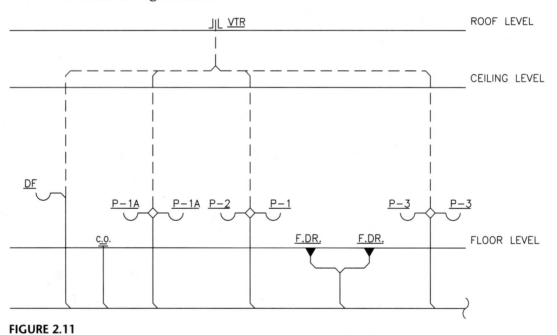

FIGURE 2.11

8. a. total fall: 345 ft $\times$ ¼-in. fall/ft + 18 in. = 86.25 in. + 18 in. = **104¼ in.** or **8 ft 8¼ in.**

    b. total fall: 345 ft $\times$ ⅛-in. fall/ft + 18 in. = 43.125 in. + 18 in. = **61⅛ in.** or **5 ft 1⅛ in.**

9. Total DFU: water closets: 2 (34 @ 6 DFU ea.) = 408 DFU

                lavatory sinks: 2 (16 @ 1 DFU ea.) = 32 DFU

                mop sinks: 2 (1 @ 2 DFU ea.) =   4 DFU (used wash

                                                                                 sink)

                                                                —————

                                                               444 DFU

    (a) **5 in.**, (b) **6 in.**

10. Using an assumed limit of 10 fixtures per VTR:

    total number of fixtures: 2(34 + 16 + 1) = 102

    number of VTRs = 102/10 = 10.2 or 11.

    Depending upon the proximity of one rest room to the other, we might need 6 VTRs per room for a total of **12 VTRs.**

APPENDIX A

Estimating Demand versus gpm

TABLE FOR ESTIMATING DEMAND

SUPPLY SYSTEMS PREDOMINANTLY FOR FLUSH TANKS			SUPPLY SYSTEMS PREDOMINANTLY FOR FLUSH VALVES		
Load	Demand		Load	Demand	
(Water supply fixture units)	(Gallons per minute)	(Cubic feet per minute)	(Water supply fixture units)	(Gallons per minute)	(Cubic feet per minute)
1	3.0	0.04104			
2	5.0	0.0684			
3	6.5	0.86892			
4	8.0	1.06944			
5	9.4	1.256592	5	15.0	2.0052
6	10.7	1.430376	6	17.4	2.326032
7	11.8	1.577424	7	19.8	2.646364
8	12.8	1.711104	8	22.2	2.967696
9	13.7	1.831416	9	24.6	3.288528
10	14.6	1.951728	10	27.0	3.60936
11	15.4	2.058672	11	27.8	3.716304
12	16.0	2.13888	12	28.6	3.823248
13	16.5	2.20572	13	29.4	3.930192
14	17.0	2.27256	14	30.2	4.037136
15	17.5	2.3394	15	31.0	4.14408
16	18.0	2.90624	16	31.8	4.241024
17	18.4	2.459712	17	32.6	4.357968
18	18.8	2.513184	18	33.4	4.464912
19	19.2	2.566656	19	34.2	4.571856
20	19.6	2.620128	20	35.0	4.6788
25	21.5	2.87412	25	38.0	5.07984
30	23.3	3.114744	30	42.0	5.61356
35	24.9	3.328632	35	44.0	5.88192
40	26.3	3.515784	40	46.0	6.14928
45	27.7	3.702936	45	48.0	6.41664
50	29.1	3.890088	50	50.0	6.684
60	32.0	4.27776	60	54.0	7.21872
70	35.0	4.6788	70	58.0	7.75344
80	38.0	5.07984	80	61.2	8.181216
90	41.0	5.48088	90	64.3	8.595624
100	43.5	5.81508	100	67.5	9.0234
120	48.0	6.41664	120	73.0	9.75864
140	52.5	7.0182	140	77.0	10.29336
160	57.0	7.61976	160	81.0	10.82808
180	61.0	8.15448	180	85.5	11.42964
200	65.0	8.6892	200	90.0	12.0312
225	70.0	9.3576	225	95.5	12.76644
250	75.0	10.0260	250	101.0	13.50168
275	80.0	10.6944	275	104.5	13.96956
300	85.0	11.3628	300	108.0	14.43744
400	105.0	14.0364	400	127.0	16.97736
500	124.0	16.57632	500	143.0	19.11624
750	170.0	22.7256	750	177.0	23.66136
1,000	208.0	27.80544	1,000	208.0	27.80544
1,250	239.0	31.94952	1,250	239.0	31.94952
1,500	269.0	35.95992	1,500	269.0	35.95992
1,750	297.0	39.70296	1,750	297.0	39.70296

TABLE FOR ESTIMATING DEMAND—(Continued)

SUPPLY SYSTEMS PREDOMINANTLY FOR FLUSH TANKS			SUPPLY SYSTEMS PREDOMINANTLY FOR FLUSH VALVES		
Load	Demand		Load	Demand	
(Water supply fixture units)	(Gallons per minute)	(Cubic feet per minute)	(Water supply fixture units)	(Gallons per minute)	(Cubic feet per minute)
2,000	325.0	43.446	2,000	325.0	43.446
2,500	380.0	50.7984	2,500	380.0	50.7984
3,000	433.0	57.88344	3,000	433.0	57.88344
4,000	535.0	70.182	4,000	525.0	70.182
5,000	593.0	79.27224	5,000	593.0	79.27224

For **SI:** 1 gpm = 3.785 L/m, 1 cfm = 0.4719 L/s.

Source: Courtesy of International Code Council. Reprinted from International Plumbing Code 1997 with permission.

APPENDIX B

Table of Pipe Sizes Based on 4 psi Pressure Loss per 100 Feet of Run

Pipe Size (in.)	Recommended Material	wsfu range (*flush tank*)	wsfu range (*flush valve*)
½	copper	0–2	n/a
¾	copper	3–6	n/a
1	copper	7–17	n/a
1¼	copper	18–30	0–5
1½	copper	31–60	6–17
2	copper	61–225	18–110
2½	black steel	226–335	111–200
3	black steel	336–640	201–555
4	black steel	641–2000	556–2000

APPENDIX C

Pressure Loss
in Smooth Pipe

FRICTION LOSS LBS. PER SQ. IN. HEAD PER 100ft. LENGTH

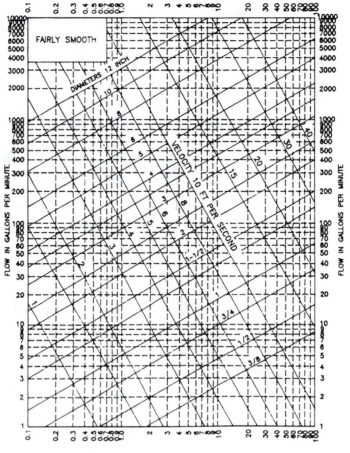

FRICTION LOSS LBS. PER SQ. IN. HEAD PER 100ft. LENGTH

FRICTION LOSS IN FAIRLY SMOOTH PIPE[a]

For **SI:** 1 inch = 25.4 mm, 1 foot = 304.8 mm, 1 gpm = 3.785 L/m, 1 psi head per 100-foot
length = 2.26 kPa head per 10 m length, 1 foot per second = 0.305 m/s.

[a] This chart applies to smooth new steel (fairly smooth) pipe and to actual diameters of
standard-weight pipe.

Source: Courtesy of International Code Council. Reprinted from International Plumbing Code 1997 with permission.

APPENDIX D

Building Drains and Sewers and Horizontal Fixture Branches and Stacks

BUILDING DRAINS AND SEWERS

DIAMETER OF PIPE (inches)	MAXIMUM NUMBER OF DRAINAGE FIXTURE UNITS CONNECTED TO ANY PORTION[a] OF THE BUILDING DRAIN OR THE BUILDING SEWER, INCLUDING BRANCHES OF THE BUILDING DRAIN			
	1/16 inch	1/8 inch	1/4 inch	1/2 inch
1 1/4			1	1
1 1/2			3	3
2			21	26
2 1/2			24	31
3		36[b]	42[b]	50[b]
4		180	216	250
5		390	480	575
6		700	840	1,000
8	1,400	1,600	1,920	2,300
10	2,500	2,900	3,500	4,200
12	2,900	4,600	5,600	6,700
15	7,000	8,300	10,000	12,000

For SI: 1 inch = 25.4 mm, 1 inch per foot = 0.0833 mm/m.

[a] Includes branches of the building drain. The minimum size of any building drain serving a water closet shall be 3 inches.

[b] Not more than three water closets.

Source: Courtesy of International Code Council. Reprinted from International Plumbing Code 1997 with permission.

HORIZONTAL FIXTURE BRANCHES AND STACKS[a]

DIAMETER OF PIPE (inches)	MAXIMUM NUMBER OF DRAINAGE FIXTURE UNITS (dfu)			
	Total for a horizontal branch	Stacks[b]		
		Total discharge into one branch interval	Total for stack of three branch intervals or less	Total for stack greater than three branch intervals
1 1/2	3	2	4	8
2	6	6	10	24
2 1/2	12	9	20	42
3	20[d]	20[d]	48	72
4	160	90	240	500
5	360	200	540	1,100
6	620	350	960	1,900
8	1,400	600	2,200	3,600
10	2,500	1,000	3,800	5,600
12	3,900	1,500	6,000	8,400
15	7,000	Footnote c	Footnote c	Footnote c

For SI: 1 inch = 25.4 mm.

[a] Does not include branches of the building drain. Refer to Table 713.1(1).

[b] Stacks shall be sized based on the total accumulated connected load at each story or branch interval. As the total accumulated connected load decreases, stacks are permitted to be reduced in size. Stack diameters shall not be reduced to less than one-half of the diameter of the largest stack size required.

[c] Sizing load based on design criteria.

[d] Not more than three water closets.

Source: Courtesy of International Code Council. Reprinted from International Plumbing Code 1997 with permission.

APPENDIX E

Size and Developed Length of Vent Stacks and Vent Pipes

SIZE AND DEVELOPED LENGTH OF STACK VENTS AND VENT STACKS

SIZE OF SOIL OR WASTE STACK (inches)	DRAINAGE FIXTURE UNITS (dfu) CONNECTED	MAXIMUM DEVELOPED LENGTH OF VENT (feet)								
		Diameter of vent required (inches)								
		1¼	1½	2	2½	3	4	5	6	8
1¼	2	30	—	—	—	—	—	—	—	—
1½	8	50	150	—	—	—	—	—	—	—
1½	10	30	100	—	—	—	—	—	—	—
2	12	30	75	200	—	—	—	—	—	—
2	20	26	50	150	—	—	—	—	—	—
2½	42	—	30	100	300	—	—	—	—	—
3	10	—	30	100	200	600	—	—	—	—
3	30	—	—	60	200	500	—	—	—	—
3	60	—	—	50	80	400	—	—	—	—
4	100	—	—	35	100	260	1,000	—	—	—
4	200	—	—	30	90	250	900	—	—	—
4	500	—	—	20	70	180	700	—	—	—
5	200	—	—	—	35	80	350	1,000	—	—
5	500	—	—	—	30	70	300	900	—	—
5	1,100	—	—	—	20	50	200	700	—	—
6	350	—	—	—	25	50	200	400	1,300	—
6	620	—	—	—	15	30	125	300	1,100	—
6	960	—	—	—	—	24	100	250	1,000	—
6	1,900	—	—	—	—	20	70	200	700	—
8	600	—	—	—	—	—	50	150	500	1,300
8	1,400	—	—	—	—	—	40	100	400	1,200
8	2,200	—	—	—	—	—	30	80	350	1,100
8	3,600	—	—	—	—	—	25	60	250	800
10	1,000	—	—	—	—	—	—	75	125	1,000
10	2,500	—	—	—	—	—	—	50	100	500
10	3,800	—	—	—	—	—	—	30	80	350
10	5,600	—	—	—	—	—	—	25	60	250

For **SI:** 1 inch = 25.4 mm, 1 foot = 304.8 mm.

Source: Courtesy of International Code Council. Reprinted from International Plumbing Code 1997 with permission.

APPENDIX F

Using the PipeSizer and SaniSizer Programs

The PipeSizer v1.0 program is designed to assist the user in the performance of basic domestic water pipe sizing computations. This program will perform the following functions based on the use of schedule 40 pipe using a pressure drop of 4 psi per 100 feet of pipe:

Determines the appropriate nominal pipe size based upon PFU demand

Adjusts pipe size for primarily flush valve or flush tank systems

Provides water supply flow rate range in gpm for each branch sized

Recommends the appropriate material (copper or steel) for the given pipe size

Writes all final piping data to a data file with a (.pip) extension

To activate the PipeSizer program, simply install it onto your computer using the following procedure:

You may install the PipeSizer program on any drive or in any directory that you choose to. To install the program:

1. Insert the 3¼-in. diskette into your matching diskette drive.

2. At the DOS prompt type COPY *X*:PIPE.* *Y* (where X is your diskette drive letter designation and Y is the destination drive) to copy into your current directory **OR** in Windows copy all "PIPE" files using the File Manager.

3. To run the PipeSizer program, type PIPE at the DOS prompt or double-click on PIPE.EXE in your Windows 3.x File Manager or Windows 95 Explorer **OR** by selecting "File" from the Windows Program Manager, then "Run," then typing PIPE, and clicking on "OK."

You may also access the PIPE.BAS file (written in QBASIC) using the MS-DOS QBASIC program editor.

The PipeSizer program creates a data file when it is run that stores all of the information that you enter into the computer while using the program. These files are automatically given the extension ".PIP," and they will be saved in the current working directory.

The SaniSizer v1.0 program is designed to assist the user in the performance of basic sanitary pipe sizing computations. This program will perform the following functions:

Determines the size sanitary waste pipe needed for a given application based upon a ¼-inch fall per foot standard when given the total DFU requirement

Provides the appropriate size pipe needed for horizontal branches that tie directly into fixtures

Supplies a warning that all water closet drain pipes must have a minimum nominal size of 3 inches

Accurately sizes all main pipes up to 3500 DFU (10 inches) and branches up to 1400 DFU (8 inches)

Writes all final drain pipe data to a data file with an (.san) extension

To activate the SaniSizer program, simply install it onto your computer using the following procedure:

You may install the SaniSizer program on any drive or in any directory that you choose to. To install SaniSizer:

1. Insert the 3¼-in. diskette into your matching diskette drive.

2. At the DOS prompt type COPY *X*:SANI.* *Y* (where *X* is your diskette drive letter designation and *Y* is the destination drive) to copy into your current directory **OR** in Windows copy all "SANI" files using the File Manager.

3. To run the SaniSizer program, type SANI at the DOS prompt or double-click on SANI.EXE in your Windows 3.x File Manager or Windows 95 Explorer **OR** by selecting "File" from the Windows Program Manager, then "Run," then typing SANI, and clicking on "OK."

You may also access the SANI.BAS file (written in QBASIC) using the MS-DOS QBASIC program editor.

The SaniSizer program creates a data file when it is run that stores all of the information that you enter into the computer while using the program. These files are automatically given the extension ".SAN," and they will be saved in the current working directory.

Appendix G

Interpolation

The process of interpolation may be used to find an intermediate value not provided by a chart or table. This process assumes a linear relationship exists between related values as they change. What this means is that if one value changes by 10 units, then the corresponding value will also change by 10 units. A linear relationship will plot as a straight line on a graph.

To illustrate a linear relationship, let's assume that you have $5000 in a savings account. Periodically, you add $100 to the account. The chart below illustrates this relationship.

Total Added	Account Balance
0	$5000
$100	$5100
$200	$5200
$300	$5300
$400	$5400
$500	$5500

Each time $100 is added to the "Total Added" column the account balance increases by $100. If we plot this relationship on a graph we get the results shown in Figure G.1.

However, most engineering data charts are not based on linear relationships. This makes it difficult to "guess" at intermediate values not provided in a chart. Let us use as our next example the relationship between wsfu demand and gpm. The chart shows loads from 100 wsfu to 200 wsfu.

Load (wsfu)	gpm
100	43.5
120	48.0
140	52.5
160	57.0
180	61.0
200	65.0

FIGURE G.1

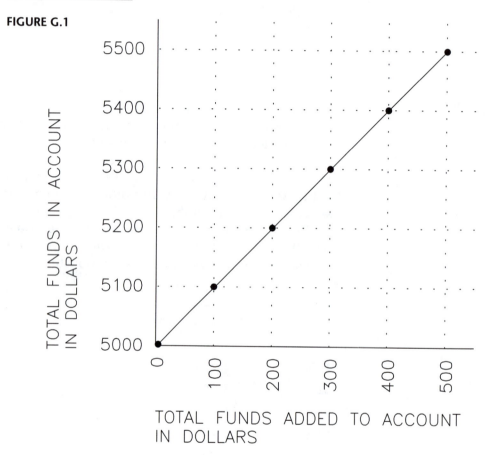

The process for computing equivalent gpm ratings for intermediate wsfu values is explained in Part I of this text. However, this process cannot be used to find corresponding wsfu values for a given intermediate gpm flow rate.

To determine a missing intermediate value by interpolation, we need to consider both chart values immediate above and below the given value.

For example, what if we need to find the equivalent of 165 wsfu in gpm? First, we set up a chart like the one shown below using a variable for the missing value.

FIGURE G.2

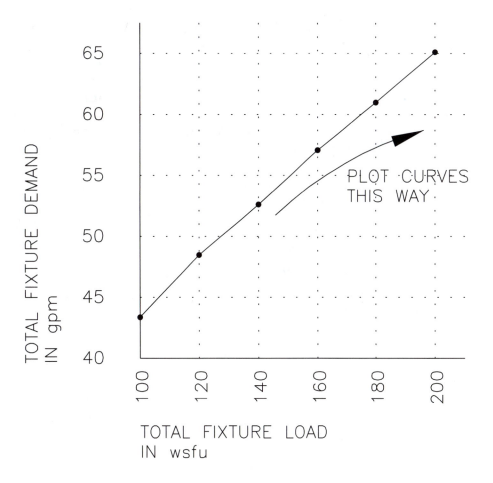

165 wfsu = ?gpm

wsfu	gpm
160	57.0
165	x
180	61.0

Next, we need to set up a formula that represents the fraction between the low and high values at which the intermediate value is located. The result is:

$$\frac{165 - 160}{180 - 160} = \frac{5}{20} = \frac{1}{4}$$

Because 165 wsfu is ¼ of the way between 160 wsfu and 180 wsfu, the unknown value x for gpm must also be close to the same location between 57.0 wsfu and 61.0 wsfu. Therefore:

$$\Delta x = ¼ (61.0 - 57.0) = 1 \text{ gpm}$$

If we add the change in gpm (Δx) to the low gpm value, we find:

$$x = 57.0 + \Delta x$$
$$= 57.0 + 1$$
$$= \textbf{58 gpm}$$

The method shown below combines this procedure into a single expression:

$$x = \frac{165 - 160}{180 - 160}(61.0 - 57.0) + 57.0$$
$$x = \frac{5}{20}(4.0) + 57.0$$
$$x = 1 + 57.0$$
$$x = \textbf{58.0 gpm}$$

APPENDIX H

Unit Conversions and Useful Formulas

1 CFM = 0.0283 m³/min
1 CFH = 0.0283 m³/hr
1 fpm = 0.3048 m/min
1 fps = 0.3048 m/sec

Density of water: 62.4 lb/ft³, 0.801 kg/m³
Density of air: 0.081 lb/ft³, 0.001 kg/m³

°C = 5/9(°F − 32)
°F = 9°C/5 + 32

1 lb = 16 oz
1 kg = 2.21 lb
1 gal = 8 lb
1 gal = 231 in.³
1 gal = 0.137 ft³

1 ft = 12 in. = 0.3048 m
1 yd = 3 ft = 0.914 m

1 ft² = 144 in.²
1 ft² = 0.093 m²
1 yd² = 9 ft²
1 yd² = 0.836 m²

1 ft³ = 1728 in.³
1 ft³ = 0.0283 m³

1 psi = 70.293 g/cm³
1 psi = 144 psf
1 psi = 702 kg/m²
1 psf = 4.875 kg/m²

$A = s^2$ (square)
$A = lw$ (rectangle)
$A = \pi r^2$ (circle)
$A = \frac{1}{4}\pi d^2$ (circle)

$V = s^3$ (square)
$V = lw\,h$ (box)
$V = \pi r^2 h$ (cylinder)
$V = \frac{1}{4}\pi d^2 h$ (cylinder)

h = height
l = length
r = radius
s = side length
w = width

FRACTIONS TO DECIMALS
⅛ = 0.1250
³⁄₁₆ = 0.1875
¼ = 0.2500
⁵⁄₁₆ = 0.3125
⅜ = 0.3750
⁷⁄₁₆ = 0.4375

165

FRACTIONS TO DECIMALS
½   = 0.5000
⁹⁄₁₆ = 0.5625
⅝   = 0.6250
¹¹⁄₁₆ = 0.6875
¾   = 0.7500
¹³⁄₁₆ = 0.8125
⅞   = 0.8750
¹³⁄₁₆ = 0.9375

°C   = degrees Celsius
fps = feet per second
fpm = feet per minute
°F   = degrees Fahrenheit
n   = number, quantity
p   = pressure
psi = pounds per square inch
psf = pounds per square foot
V = volume
v = velocity
π = pi (3.14159...)

GLOSSARY

ADA—Americans with Disabilities Act. A nationwide set of regulations that governs the installation, operation, and maintenance standards of all public and private facilities that are designed to be handicapped accessible.

adapter—This type of fitting is commonly used to attach pipe runs to appliances where the pipe and/or thread size and type may differ.

ambient—Conditions existing naturally outside the building or system.

ATC—Automatic temperature control. This is an electronic device that is used to operate valving and regulate fluid flow based upon the temperature of the water in a domestic water system at certain points along its path.

backflow—A condition in which material flows in the wrong direction in a sanitary line.

beam clamp—A supporting device that is used to attach a pipe hanger to a structural beam in a building.

Bernoulli principle—Fluid flow in a given direction over a surface reduces air pressure.

bushing—A type of coupling that has a variety of applications. Bushings can be used to connect pipes having different thread or connection types, different sizes, or male and female ends.

ceiling flange—A supporting device that is used to attach a pipe hanger to a flat surface located overhead.

chase—A vertical opening inside or near a wall that is designed to allow space for piping to run from one floor to another.

chiller—A refrigeration unit that is designed to lower the temperature of a cold domestic water supply, usually for drinking.

clean out—Capped opening that allows direct access to sanitary pipe for removal of obstructions.

coupling—A short segment of pipe that is used to connect two larger segments of pipe.

developed length—The length of vent pipe measured from fixture to the VTR.

DFUs—Drainage fixture units. Arbitrary units used to size sanitary/vent pipe based on waste flow volume.

dielectric fitting—Prevents low-level electricity flow between ferrous (containing iron) and nonferrous metals used in piping. This electrical flow could cause slow decomposition of the piping if not prevented.

domestic water—Water that is suitable for human contact and/or consumption.

drain—An opening at the base of a plumbing fixture that is designed to allow the fluid contents of that fixture to escape.

eye wash—A fixture used to flush a person's eyes with water under moderate pressure. Commonly located on factory floors or wherever possibility exists of chemicals or foreign matter entering someone's eyes.

fitting—A device used to connect two segments of pipe. Fittings may also be used to change the direction and/or size of a pipe run.

fixture—A plumbing device that utilizes water delivered by the supply system.

flange—Used to connect pipes or fittings in higher pressure applications.

floor drain—Used to allow water that may accumulate on floor to escape into sanitary system.

flush tank—Describes a fixture that uses water stored in a tank in order to flush its waste contents.

flush valve—Describes a fixture that relies on the incoming water pressure in order to flush its waste contents.

gpm—Gallons per minute. The common English unit for fluid volumetric flow.

gravometric—Driven by gravity.

hanger—A mounting device used to suspend piping from an overhead structure.

hose bibb—A water faucet with external threading for connecting to a hose.

insulation—A wrap or blanket that is used to prevent or retard heat transfer through the walls of a pipe.

invert elevation—The elevation to the bottom of an uninsulated pipe or to the bottom of the insulation of an insulated pipe.

IPC—International Plumbing Code.

lavatory—More commonly known as a hand sink or bathroom sink.

manufacturer's specifications—Specific information about a product provided by the manufacturer at the time of purchase. This information may include connection sizes, operating conditions, maintenance schedules, and limitations of the product.

match line—In drafting, a reference line showing where two parts of a building meet.

mixing valve—A valve that is used to blend hot and cold water supplies to achieve a desired supply temperature.

pfu—**Plumbing fixture units.** Similar to *wsfu*. This particular unit has been replaced in recent years by the wsfu used in the International Plumbing Code.

pipe—A hollow metal or plastic tube that is used to direct the flow of a fluid.

pipe anchor—A type of pipe support that is designed to prevent motion of the pipe.

pipe guide—These devices are used to maintain pipe direction and alignment.

pipe shield—This device is used to protect the pipe insulation from damage at points where the insulated pipe is being supported.

plumbing fixture schedule—A table that lists all of the plumbing fixtures used in a building along with additional useful information about each fixture.

polybutylene—A durable plastic that is used primarily in domestic water supply systems. This plastic can serve the same purpose as copper piping in most domestic water applications.

primer—An outside source of water used to keep a trap clean and moist.

PRS—Pressure reducing station. An assembly of valves and fittings that is designed to reduce the pressure of the domestic water from a utility main to a level that can be safely utilized by a building system.

PVC—Polyvinyl chloride. This plastic exists in several compounds and is commonly used for sanitary piping, vent piping, and storm drain piping.

reducer—A fitting that is designed to connect two pipes of different diameters.

riser clamp—These pipe supporting devices are used to attach vertical runs of pipe to a wall or other stationary structure.

riser diagram—A schematic that is used by designers to show the routing and order of connection in a piped system.

sanitary plan—A floor plan with sanitary waste piping and vent piping superimposed.

sanitary waste system—A plumbing system used to remove wastewater and other waste products from plumbing fixtures in building.

sanitary waste vent system—System that allows free flow of gases between sanitary pipe and outside of building.

siphonage—A vacuum-like effect in a sanitary line that causes backflow.

snake—A tool used by plumbers to break up blockages inside a sanitary pipe.

soil stack—A vent pipe connected directly to a water closet or its adjacent sanitary line.

strainer—A filtration device that is used to remove small solid particles from a water stream inside a piped system.

takeoff—Any pipe connection to a main run that uses water from that run.

tie-in—The point at which a vertical vent pipe connects to a horizontal vent pipe.

trap—A bend in sanitary pipe designed to improve the flow of large blockages.

union—A removable connection that is used near appliances or devices that may need to be removed for service or replacement.

utility main—A pipe, usually located underground, that is supplied with water by the local water utility company.

valve—A device that is used to control or regulate the flow of a fluid through a pipe.

vent pipe—A pipe designed to allow the free flow of air and gases between sanitary piping and the outside of the building.

Venturi effect—A drop in pressure results from a fluid rushing by an opening.

volumetric flow—A measure of fluid flow rate that involves determining the volume of water (usually in gallons) that flows through a pipe or fixture during a unit of time (usually one minute).

VTR—Vent through roof.

water closet—More commonly known as a toilet.

wsfu—Water supply fixture units. An arbitrary scale of units that roughly corresponds to the volumetric flow demand of a fixture.

BIBLIOGRAPHY

1. International Code Council, Inc. *The International Plumbing Code 1997*. Country Club Hills, NJ: BOCA International, Inc.; Whittier, CA: International Conference of Building Officials; Birmingham, AL: Southern Building Code Congress International, 1997.

2. Putnam, Robert. Builder's Comprehensive Dictionary. Reston, VA: Craftsman Book, 1989.

3. Merriam Webster's Collegiate Dictionary, 10th ed. Springfield: Merriam Webster, 1996.

4. Boyce/Margolis/Slade. *Mathematics for Technical and Vocational Students*. Upper Saddle River, NJ: Prentice Hall, 1989.

5. Thomas, Paul I. *The Contractor's Field Guide*. Upper Saddle River, NJ: Prentice Hall, 1991.

6. Traister, John E. *Planning and Designing Plumbing Systems*. Carlsbad, CA: Craftsman Book Company, 1983.

INDEX

3746- -

NOTICE

This book contains
computer disks.
Remove before charging.

This book contains __1__
computer disk(s)
in the pocket inside the
book cover.
Please check the pocket
before discharging.